TANKS

TANKS

Richard Humble

Arthur Barker Limited

For Wenny

Designed by John Rushton Associates

Printed in Great Britain.

Photographic Acknowledgments

The illustrations in this book are supplied or reproduced by kind permission of the following:
Associated Press, London 110–11; Bavaria-Verlag, Munich *118, 126*; Bildarchiv Preussischer
Kulturbesitz, Berlin 30, 56–7, 63, 65T, 76, 80B; British Aircraft Corporation 137; Bundesministerium
der Verteidigung 129B; Camera Press, London 85, 87T, 99; Central Office of Information, Crown
Copyright *122–3*, 130, 136; ECP Armées 36–7; Eupra Press Service, Munich 81B; Fox Photos,
London *46–7*; Fotokhronika Tass, Moscow endpapers; Imperial War Museum, London 14, 21, 23,
24, 26T, 33, 50, 61, 62, 65C, 65B, 73, 77, 86, 87BL, 103; Keystone Press, London 87BR, 100TL,
113TR, 113C, 113B, 135; Kunsthistorischen Museum, Vienna 10; Mary Evans Picture Library,
London 12; J. G. Moore Collection, London 66–7; Novosti Press Agency, London 60B, 91T, 92–3,
96, 102, 132–3; Popperfoto, London 28T, 29T, 40, 113TL, 117, 138; Profile Publications Ltd,
Windsor *34–5, 38–9, 42–3T, 70–1, 74–5, 78–9, 114–15, 119, 127*; RAC Tank Museum, Bovington
32B, 41, 44, 45, 58, 59, 100TR, 100B, 101B, 101T, 106, 107, 120, 121, 124, 125; Radio Times Hulton
Picture Library, London 51, 112–13; Ronan Picture Library, Loughton 6, 9L, 9R, 9B; Scala,
Florence 11; Suddeutscher Verlag, Munich 2–3, 16–17, 26B, 28B, 29B, 31, 32T, 48–9, 52T, 52–3B,
53T, 53B, 54T, 54B, 55, 60T, 60C, 72, 80T, 81T, 88, 91B, 95T, 95B, 97, 104, 105, 139; Ullstein
Bilderdienst, Berlin 98; US Army 129T; Weidenfeld and Nicolson Archives 82–3; Wiener Library
(photograph by Derrick Witty) 42–3B.
Italics indicate colour illustrations
Picture research by Bridget Gascoyne
Line drawings by John Thompson.

Contents

1 The Dream of Juggernaut
page 6

4 The Coming of the Panzers
page 48

7 The Defeat of the Panzers
page 92

2 A Weapon is Born
page 16

5 The Triumph of the Panzers
page 56

8 Allied Victory, Cold War
page 110

3 Forgotten Lessons
page 36

6 America and Russia
page 82

9 The Tank in the Nuclear Age
page 132

Appendices   **Further Reading**   **Index**
page 140   *page 142*   *page 143*

1 The Dream of Juggernaut

I n December 1903, eighteen months after the treaty of Vereeniging wrote *finis* to the Boer War, H.G. Wells published another of his short-story sketches of the shape of things to come in *The Strand Magazine*. Obviously inspired by the inconclusive clashes of the recent war in South Africa, this story – entitled *The Land Ironclads* – told of the shattering of trench-bound deadlock on a battlefield by the co-ordinated use of a revolutionary weapon: a self-propelled armoured fighting vehicle against which no orthodox military defence could endure.

'The thing had come into such a position as to enfilade the trench, which was empty now, so far as he could see, except for two or three crouching knots of men and the tumbled dead. Behind it, across the plain, it had scored the grass with a train of linked impressions, like the dotted tracings sea-things leave in sand. Left and right of that track dead men and wounded men were scattered – men it had picked off as they fled back from their advanced positions in the search-light glare from the invader's lines. And now it lay with its head projecting a little over the trench it had won, as if it were a single sentient thing planning the next phase of the attack ...'

Twenty-seven years later, Winston Churchill, putting the finishing touches to his own history of the First World War, generously paid tribute to the vision of H.G. Wells. *The Land Ironclads,* wrote Churchill, 'had practically exhausted the possibilities of imagination in this sphere'. But Churchill also pointed out that there was nothing intrinsically new about the concept of a self-propelled armoured vehicle capable of traversing and dominating a battlefield – the stratagem, or weapon, which we know today as 'a tank'. In fact the idea went back for centuries and had first taken shape during the later Middle Ages.

Reduced to its essentials, victory in combat has always stemmed from being able to repulse the enemy's attacks while hitting the enemy harder than he hits you, and the result – from the first primitive shield and armour to the anti-missile-missile of today – is built-in escalation. The effect of the enemy's weapons must be cancelled out by your protection, while your weapons must penetrate *his* protection – stone blunts scissors, scissors cut paper. In this contest personal armour was never, at best, more than a partial solution. Two fully-armoured mounted knights, fighting by the rules of chivalry and thus not trying to disable each other's horses, could do very little damage to each other in hand-to-hand combat. But an ordinary foot soldier, pouncing on a dismounted knight whose horse had been unchivalrously shot, could easily pin the knight down by sitting on his chest and kill him simply by pushing a dagger through the helmet-slit.

For centuries an enclosed wagon, a small mobile fortress trundling across the battlefield with men fighting unscathed from inside, was an obvious dream – but equally obvious was the fact that it would have to be drawn by horses and could thus be immobilized by the simple expedient of shooting the horses. But the introduction of windmills in the early fourteenth century seemed to offer a way out. The wind provided a source of power which no enemy could neutralize and the first attempt to design a wind-powered battle-wagon is represented by the sketches of an Italian physician, Guido da Vigevano, in 1335. It was never a practical proposition – its small wheelbase could never have coped with irregular terrain, while it was so top-heavy that the hurricane which would have been needed to move it would have toppled it over where it stood first. For all that, da Vigevano's idea was the first recognizable essay in self-propelled fighting vehicle design.

Cannon also appeared in the fourteenth century and developed steadily from their crude, static beginnings. By the beginning of the fifteenth century light-weight portable cannon were on the verge of acceptance; taken one step further and reduced to a size which one man could manhandle onto a rest, they became

PREVIOUS PAGES Idea for an armoured fighting vehicle, Renaissance style, by Roberto Valturio. This absurdity nevertheless recommends fire-power in the best shooting position (the dart-firing cannon), self-propulsion from inside (by rope and pulley – but who fixes the rope?), and versatility in the primitive bridge-laying gadget. Note also the hull-mounted cannon, making this a surrealist early design for a bridge-laying Char-B (see p. 41).

the first crude muskets. The punch and range (if not the accuracy) of these early light cannon suggested new possibilities; and during the Hussite wars in Bohemia (1420–33) cannon fire-power gave a startling new twist to the old dream of the battle-wagon.

The man responsible was the leader of the Hussite freedom-fighters, John Žižka. He used tough farm carts to transport troops and light cannon. These battle-wagons moved in formation, covering each other's blind spots. When they halted they were backed together to form squares and fastened together to

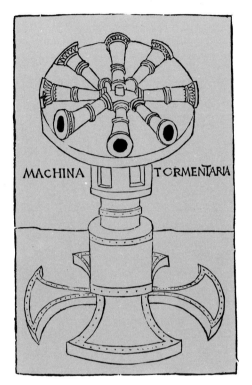

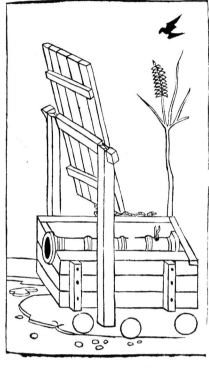

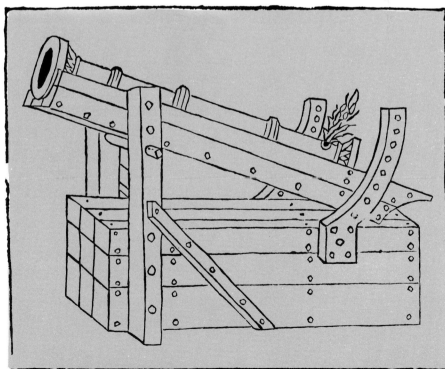

More modern tank essentials grasped by Valturio: (above left) a 360° arc of fire for the gun; (above right) mobile cannon with protection for the gunners (shades of the Hussite battle-wagons); (right) and elevating gear to get maximum range and accuracy from the cannon.

Painting by Nikolaus Glockenthon of an Austrian 'war chariot', about 1505. Here the motive power is human and there is an early example of a sloped armoured shield to protect the gunner (the 'glacis plate' of a modern tank). The barbed spears are to keep assailants out of killing range of the crew – one of the functions performed by a modern tank's machine-guns.

create a formidable strongpoint, packed with troops and bristling with cannon. This defensive formation could be broken up and the wagons set on the move again with remarkable speed.

Fire-power; close formation; mobility; the strong defensive position or 'leaguer' – these were elements of tank warfare which were over five hundred years ahead of their time, and Žižka's battle-wagons won an impressive string of victories for the Hussite armies. For all that, they did not inspire any widespread imitation. Inventors, such as the Italian Roberto Valturio, toyed less successfully with the battle-wagon idea later in the fifteenth century; but Žižka's formula went into limbo.

The Renaissance which ushered in the sixteenth century saw a tremendous interest in harnessing science for the more efficient waging of war, and one of the most famous 'ancestors of the tank' was suggested among the innumerable sketches of Leonardo da Vinci (1500). His conical 'tank' looked impressively futuristic. Leonardo was in fact using one of the oldest principles in the history of armour, namely that a sloping surface is best for deflecting blows or missiles. Leonardo's 'tank' had pierced weapon-slits for the defence of the eight-man crew, who were to drive the vehicle by hand – the transmission being by means of geared crankshafts. These vehicles (which never saw the light of day, let alone appeared on a battlefield) were emphatically not designed for speed or hitting-power. They were rather deliberate oddities to crack enemy morale, penetrating hostile ranks like invulnerable beetles – and they must, Leonardo stressed, be immediately followed up by occupying infantry.

For the next two hundred years after Leonardo, individuals still tinkered with the elusive concept of the fighting vehicle, but were repeatedly foiled by the propulsion problem. Any fool could design an impregnable closed vehicle – but how could it be used if it could not be moved from inside? The harnessing of steam, first for shipping and soon after for railway locomotives, promised another breakthrough in the nineteenth century. The first recognizable design for a steam battle vehicle came from the Briton James Cowan in the Crimean War

Leonardo da Vinci's design for a 'tank'. Impressively futuristic with its sloped armour, it was never intended to be more than a morale-cracking way of penetrating the enemy ranks, to be followed up hard and fast by orthodox infantry. The drive was hand-cranked, transmitted to the wheels by gears – a touching expression of faith in human muscle-power but less than adequate, particularly on any kind of uneven terrain.

(1854–6). Shaped like a round, hump-backed dish cover and bristling with guns, it was a cross between Boadicea's chariot and da Vinci's conical design; Cowan envisaged a ring of scythes with which to mow down enemy infantry, a bloodthirsty refinement that only made the projected vehicle look even more outlandish.

As the nineteenth century progressed there was no lack of similar designs but it became clear that steam, which could power so many machines from railway locomotives to farming machinery, was not really suitable for projected fighting vehicles. A steam engine was too big and too vulnerable for the battlefield. It needed impressive amounts of fuel and water, and when given an armoured shield thick enough to protect its vitals it became too heavy to move.

For all that, the quest for an armoured fighting vehicle was becoming more realistic as the nineteenth century drew to its close – realistic in that none of the earlier ideas (with the sole exception of Žižka's battle-wagons) had coped practically with the problem of moving a vehicle across the uneven terrain of a real battlefield. And even Žižka would have been thwarted by the trench systems used in the Crimea, in the American Civil War and every major conflict down to 1914. When designers of the later nineteenth century really began to look at what modern battlefields were like, the square and circular vehicle shapes vanished. They would not do for terrain which had been torn up by heavy shells and pitted with deep craters, let alone for crossing trenches for which a long vehicle was obviously essential. It was just as clear that the wheel was of little use: it did not grip the ground well enough, it got easily bogged down or blocked, and was not flexible enough for severely uneven terrain.

The latter problem was tackled with two ideas, both of them patented in the nineteenth century: wheels-with-feet, or 'pedrails', and endless-chain tracks with the grip provided by metal plates. By the close of the century both pedrails and tracks had been demonstrated on steam vehicles and had been proved workable and it was not clear which of the two would prove superior. H. G. Wells, impressed by the experiments of Bramah Diplock, inventor of the pedrail, chose

How the 'land ironclads' of H. G. Wells first appeared in *The Strand Magazine*, 1903.

pedrails when he wrote *The Land Ironclads* in 1903, envisaging a long vehicle for trench-crossing with rows of pedrail-wheels down the sides protected by an armoured 'skirt'.

A close read of *The Land Ironclads* shows that Wells was not being quite honest when he described the machinery. His first deliberately vague description refers to a regular engine beat and an exhaust 'squirting out little jets of steam behind'; Wells's later 'guided tour' of the interior of a fighting land iron-clad mentions that 'the air was thick with the smell of oil and petrol'. This discrepancy is no accident, it seems: H. G. Wells, normally so precise when it came to mechanical detail, seems to have been genuinely unable to make up his mind whether the steam engine or the internal combustion engine would prevail.

Wells also failed to appreciate the revolution in fire-power achieved by the coming of the machine-gun. This weapon, heralded by the crude-looking Gatling with its revolving bundle of barrels, had been in use for over thirty years. But, to be fair, the machine-gun was still an uncertain quantity in 1903: had Wells written the story in 1914, when the belt-fed Maxim gun had been adopted by nearly every army in the world, he must have given his land iron-clads machine-guns. As it was, Wells was content to arm them with sophisticated rifles, mounted in broadsides with the choice of target and rate of fire left to the discretion of the individual riflemen behind their armour. Wells, in short, did not bother to think of an armoured fighting vehicle with more hitting-power than that of a mobile squad of snipers.

Since the original successes by Gottlieb Daimler and Karl Benz in the 1880s, motor vehicles powered by internal-combustion engines had become a reality by 1903. To inventors looking for military possibilities, the first light cars and motorcycles of the 1890s and early 1900s suggested a new avenue of development: an armoured car, on wheels, which could be armed with one or more machine-guns.

The first designs for such vehicles certainly did not suggest the mass and menace of the land ironclads, and one of the most famous (that of F.R.Simms, 1890) seems irresistibly comic today. Simms produced a four-wheeled motor-cycle running on spoked wheels. Its Maxim gun poked forward through a modest slab of armour plate. The celebrated photograph of this contraption, with its bowler-hatted rider crouched grimly in the saddle, certainly helps us understand why these new ideas were not enthusiastically taken up by the military experts of the day – they tended to look too hilarious for words. Yet the inventors persisted, and by 1906 armoured cars were no longer a joke. They were being seriously developed in France, Germany, Britain and Italy, and across the Atlantic in the United States. They were generally accepted by the outbreak of war in 1914. Perhaps the soundest of all was the Rolls Royce armoured car developed from the immortal Silver Ghost, which served nobly in both world wars.

Armoured cars, however, were only a half-answer to the elusive riddle of the armoured fighting vehicle. They needed tolerably good terrain in which to operate, being as useless as any other wheeled vehicle where mud, dense obstacles or trenches were concerned. The problem which faced the engineer-designers was still the same. Which was the most efficient way to spread a vehicle's weight over boggy ground, while giving maximum flexibility over uneven ground? The endless track fitted with rectangular steel plates proved far more efficient than the circular 'feet' of the pedrail; even Diplock himself abandoned pedrail wheels in 1910 and experimented with pedrail feet mounted on a chain track.

America and Britain took the lead in designing the tracked vehicle. First off the mark were the Americans F.W.Batter (1888) and G.M.Edwards (1890), both designing practicable steam-powered vehicles that ran on tracks. British designers started by taking the big steam traction engines, which were the largest non-rail land tractors in the country, and experimenting with tracked conversions.

Between 1905 and 1912 in Britain there was an exciting period of rivalry between the firms of Hornsby and Holt which all but completed the picture. Both produced steam tracked vehicles but Hornsby's were first in the field with a petrol-engined version (1907), beating Holt's by a year. In 1908 the War Office offered a £1000 prize for a cross-country tractor which could pull a load forty miles without refuelling. Both Hornsby's and Holt's rose to the challenge, the former so efficiently that an army officer, Major Donoghue, put forward a suggestion for mounting a gun on a Hornsby tractor and casing it in armour.

This Donoghue–Hornsby variant should have been the first modern 'tank', but the project was ignored by the War Office and official interest in Britain waned swiftly. Hornsby's sold their foreign patents to Holt's in 1912; Herr Steiner, the Holt representative, persevered with determined salesmanship but the German General Staff was unimpressed. In 1914 the future for the tracked armoured fighting vehicle looked as unpromising as ever, even though so many of the traditional problems had been overcome.

It is easy to look back and condemn the military experts of 1914 for their blinkered obstinacy in rejecting the new ideas. In all fairness, the tremendous advances of the Industrial Revolution had thrown up quite as many crackpot ideas as workable projects, and if anything more. This inevitably produced a defensive scepticism towards wild-eyed inventors with outlandish machines.

Front Steering Portion pivoted at (A), enabling the steersman to lay the chain-track straight or curved in either direction at will.

Chain-Track

(A)

Horizontal Roller against side of chain for guiding the chain through the vehicle.

Four Bodies secured to main frame of vehicle so that they may move laterally to conform to a Curve in the Chain-Track when the vehicle is turning.

The Tank in full armour.

Detail of Chain-Track Underside View

Details of Chain-Track

Underside View of Tank showing small curve of chain-track and the front steering portion in position to lay a curve for turning purposes

Top view of Tank showing chain-track passing straight through the body of vehicle from sprocket at rear to the horizontal rollers in front.

Front View showing high clearance of Tank to prevent the machine from becoming bogged.

Only a deliberate research programme, planned to tackle all outstanding obstacles to the evolution of the armoured fighting vehicle, could have solved the riddle by the outbreak of the First World War – and this could not have come to pass because the actual conditions of the Western Front did not exist and were unimaginable before 1915. Europe's armies went to war in August 1914 under the assumption that artillery existed to break up the enemy's attacks and stun him in his positions, infantry existed to storm a breach in the enemy's line, and cavalry existed to flood through the breach and win the battle. Their assumption was quite natural, based on the traditional combat roles of horse, foot and guns, and they looked forward confidently to a rapid conclusion of hostilities in a matter of months.

Only when these confident hopes had been dashed by the hideous reality of the Western Front did conditions really favour the development of the armoured fighting vehicle. For the first time, it suddenly became desperately important that the dream should become a reality.

OPPOSITE Ingenious, practical, but hopelessly before its time and duly ignored: de Mole's design for an armoured vehicle, 1912. Here the salient feature is the steering, achieved by warping or 'bowing' the chain tracks instead of braking them.

2 A Weapon is Born

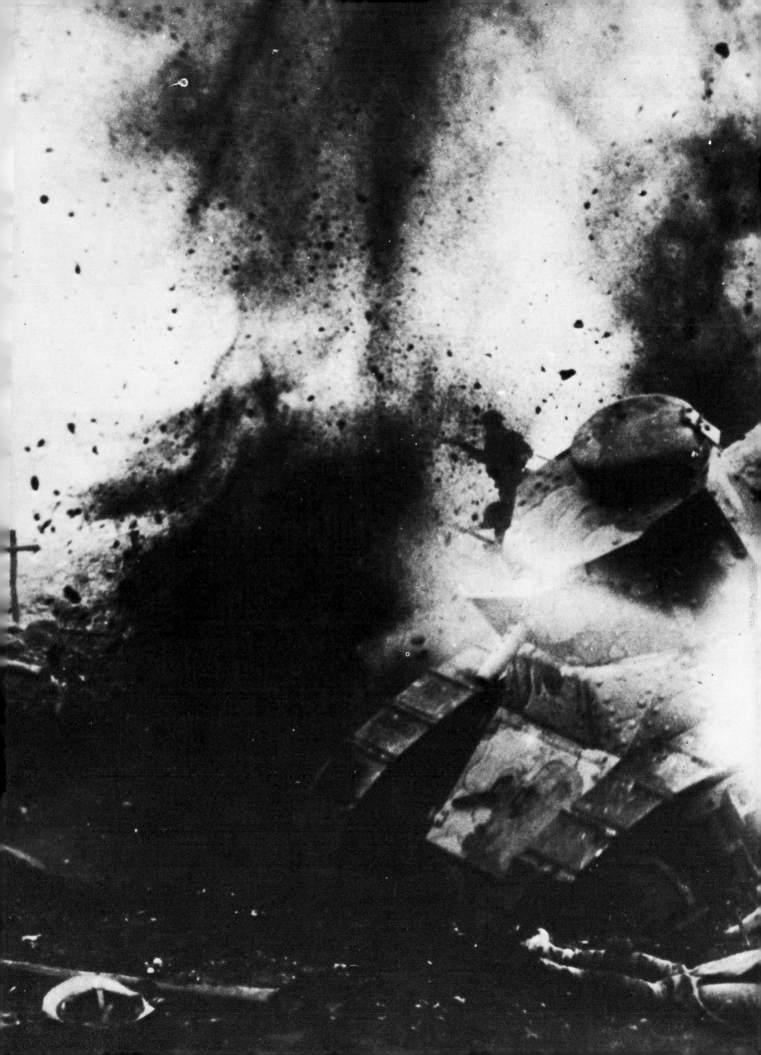

The first four months of the First World War were quite enough to stand all existing ideas of how to make war on their collective head, and the first lesson offered was the murderous effect of modern infantry weapons (repeating rifles as well as machine-guns) on massed infantry advancing in close order.

At Morhange and Sarrebourg in Lorraine, attacking precisely where they were expected, two French armies advanced chest-high to the guns in the technicolour splendour of blue tunics and scarlet trousers only to be bloodily repulsed. Meanwhile the German right-flank armies wheeled south into Belgium and northern France, colliding *en route* with the small British Expeditionary Force. At Mons and Le Cateau the British savaged the Germans with rapid rifle fire before being forced to retreat by the threat to their flanks.

When the German southward advance petered out on the River Marne (9 September 1914), there followed the so-called 'race to the sea', a north-westerly haphazard surge with each side trying to outflank the other and finally reaching the Channel in mutual deadlock. The last great battle of 1914 in the west took place when the Germans tried desperately to puncture the flimsy British screen defending the Belgian town of Ypres, and thus score a decisive breakthrough. In repeated, reckless attacks the Germans used every trick in the military book, and according to all precedents and common sense they ought to have won. They had artillery superiority and used it mercilessly. By hurling in every green, untried unit they could find, they retained manpower superiority as well and were able to keep the pressure on throughout the battle (18 October–11 November). They even flung in the crack division of the whole German army, the Prussian Guard. All was in vain. That line of muddy, exhausted British soldiers (infantrymen, dismounted cavalrymen, cooks, runners, every man in the area who could be thrown into the line with a rifle) repelled all the German attacks from a hastily-drawn seam of drainage ditches and rabbit scrapes later connected by proper trenches, largely with rifle fire supplemented by a meagre scattering of machine-guns.

After Ypres the Germans assumed the defensive in the west. They still had a full-scale war on their hands in the east against the Russian Empire, whose initial blundering invasion of East Prussia had been bloodily repulsed at Tannenberg and the Masurian Lakes. Although the German invasion of the west had failed to crush France, Belgium and the industrial northern region of France were safely under German occupation; and the Allies were to spend the next three years trying to get them back. To do this meant breaking through the line of German trenches in a decisive battle.

The Germans grasped the realities of trench warfare very rapidly. To start with they held all the high ground, the gunner's dream – even when 'high ground' only meant a barely-detectable wrinkle in the terrain. The Allies therefore had to attack uphill, towards gun positions which looked down on them. The Germans held other strong cards. The attacking Allies, in stockpiling ammunition and stores, and cramming men into the forward trenches for each new assault, could never achieve complete surprise because these preparations were so obvious. The Allies also clung to the erroneous belief that no attack had a chance of succeeding unless it was preceded by a prolonged artillery bombardment. While the guns battered away the waiting Allied troops would be told that the shell-storm was killing the Germans in droves and cutting to pieces the barbed-wire defences screening the German trenches. In fact the Germans were taking cover in deep dug-outs, waiting for the Allied guns to shift target to the German rear areas, signalling the attack. The Germans would then rush out, man their trenches, and mow down the plodding attackers with machine-gun fire. Never once did an artillery bombardment destroy enemy barbed-wire defences. And even when a section of enemy trench was badly knocked about the Germans exploited the fact that shell-holes are much easier to defend than

PREVIOUS PAGES British infantry advance behind one of the flimsy French Renault M-17s, 1917 – apparently undeterred by the spectacular destruction of the machine on the right.

to attack (a fact of battlefield life which both sides were repeatedly to forget in the Second World War).

When an Allied attack did manage to win a few hundred yards of German front-line trench after strenuous efforts and immense loss of life, it was always found that the Germans had not put all their eggs in one basket. Their defence was in depth and they could quickly throw in counter-attacks, sealing off the threatened breach almost as soon as it was made and as likely as not throwing back the surviving attackers to where they had come from. Easily ninety per cent of every attack was spent in gaining the front-line trench – but this was only the beginning if a genuine breakthrough was to be made. Beyond the German front line lay a zig-zag web of more trenches and still more trenches leading into the German rear areas, with resistance stiffening all the way. All this could make a nonsense of paper planning. At Neuve Chapelle on 10 March 1915 the British attacked with forty-eight battalions against three German battalions. In three days of bitter fighting they won the German front line but lost 12,892 officers and men in the process; and instead of making a decisive breakthrough in the direction of Lille they captured a bare thousand yards of ground. Festubert and Aubers Ridge produced even worse results in May, and so did the first so-called 'big push' at Loos (September–November 1915).

Nevertheless, the year 1915 was the one in which – at last – serious planning was initiated at official level to produce an armoured fighting vehicle which could succeed where flesh and blood seemed bound to suffer eternal failure. With the onus on the Allies to attack, and on the Germans to defend, it was to be expected that the British and French would produce the first successful armoured fighting vehicle and not the Germans. But the British and French experiments in 1915 were quite independent from each other; and in Britain all the impetus and official encouragement came not from the army but from the navy – or, to be more precise, from the fertile imagination of Winston Churchill, First Lord of the Admiralty in Asquith's government.

Churchill himself tells how it all began in *The World Crisis*:

'In the early weeks of the War the Admiralty had been asked to assume responsibility for the defence of Britain against aerial attack. This necessitated the posting on the Belgian and French coasts of Air Squadrons based on Dunkirk to attack any Zeppelin or aeroplane shed which the enemy might establish in the invaded territories. This led to the formation of armoured-car squadrons to protect the advanced bases which our naval aeroplanes might require to use. The enemy, harassed by the armoured cars, cut gaps in the roads, and I called immediately for means of bridging these gaps. Meanwhile the armoured cars began to multiply, but just as they became numerous and efficient, the trench lines on both sides reached the sea, and there was no longer any open ground for manoeuvre or any flanks to turn. As we could not go round the trenches, it was evidently necessary to go over them. Thus the Air was the first cause that took us to Dunkirk. The armoured car was the child of the air; the Tank its grandchild. This was the point which the chain of causation had reached in the second week of October 1914.'

Churchill was the first to admit that he was not the only man of vision. Since his retirement Rear-Admiral Sir Reginald Bacon, a former Director of Naval Operations, had spent five years as general manager of the Coventry Ordnance Works, which produced a third of Britain's heavy guns. In the opening fortnight of the war Bacon submitted to Churchill the idea of a 15-inch howitzer capable of use in land operations. The two men met. Bacon forecast that modern fortresses would be unable to withstand the enormous hitting-power of modern heavy artillery, and was almost immediately proved right by the destruction of the Belgian forts of Liège and Namur by the big German siege guns. Impressed, Churchill went to the War Office with the idea and with Field-Marshal Lord

Kitchener's backing secured an order for ten. With such a speedy reaction at the top the first of these monster land guns reached the British front in time to be fired at Neuve Chapelle.

This was the first step, the second being that such big guns were designed to be moved by caterpillar-tracked tractors. Bacon showed Churchill the first designs for the latter in October 1914. Churchill told Bacon to go ahead with an experimental model, but this was turned down by the army in May 1915 because it could not go down a 4-feet bank and wade through 3 feet of water (a task which, as Churchill later pointed out with no little bitterness, was not accomplished by any tank up to the end of the war).

But by the time of this rebuff an even more encouraging beginning had been made. Colonel E. D. Swinton reported from General Headquarters in France towards the end of October 1914 that such vehicles were needed at the front. His report was worked up into a paper by Colonel Maurice Hankey, Secretary of the War Council, and circulated among Cabinet ministers, Churchill included. Delighted to find outside confirmation of his own enthusiasm, Churchill wrote a letter to Prime Minister Asquith stressing the urgency of pressing ahead. Both Asquith and Lord Kitchener were keen, but the latter made the mistake (understandable in a man who virtually carried the whole weight of the war on his shoulders) of passing the problem to the army's Ordnance Department, who slew it with bureaucratic procedures and buried it in the archives.

Churchill meanwhile had a shrewd idea that the matter was not being pressed as it deserved. On 19 January he told the Director of the Air Division of the Admiralty to experiment with trench-smashing steamrollers, one of the ideas specified in Hankey's memorandum. This, like previous experimental spasms, also came to nothing, proving mechanically unfeasible – but it was equally indicative of a new pulse that had begun to beat.

One of the most important social evenings in military history, fit to rank with the Duchess of Richmond's ball on the eve of Waterloo, took place on 17 February 1915. Churchill was a key guest, and if there was anything which got the best out of him it was a congenial gathering in the company of men who knew their jobs:

'The Duke of Westminster, who commanded a squadron of armoured cars and who was himself a focus of discussion on these subjects [armoured fighting vehicles and their feasibility], invited me to dine on February 17 to meet several officers from the armoured-car squadrons. The conversation turned on cross-country armoured vehicles, and Major Hetherington, who also belonged to the armoured-car squadrons and knew of the various experiments which had been made, spoke with force and vision on the whole subject, advocating the creation of land battleships on a scale far larger than has ever been found practicable.

As a result of this conversation, I went home determined that I would give imperative orders without delay to secure the carrying forward in one form or another of the project in which I had so long believed.'

The result, three days later, was the formation of the Landships Committee of the Admiralty on Churchill's order (20 February 1915). Its president was Eustace Tennyson d'Eyncourt, Chief Constructor of the Navy, and its first task was to look into the colossal project with which Hetherington had impressed Churchill.

This was the Hetherington 'Big Wheel': 300 tons, three twin 4-inch gun turrets, powered by an 800-hp submarine engine and running on notched wheels 40 feet in diameter. Nothing if not grandiose, this project was too obviously self-defeating. Even when the wheel diameter was reduced to 15 feet it made too splendid a target, and would have taken an inordinate time to build. A wooden mock-up was begun but by June 1915 the project had been dropped.

Long before this, however, Churchill had been told of other experiments with smaller tracked vehicles, which encouraged him to make one of the biggest personal gambles of his career. Without consulting the Board of the Admiralty, the War Office, or the Treasury, he personally ordered 18 experimental vehicles at a cost of about £70,000 of public money. This was on 26 March 1915. No wonder that Churchill made enemies and was regarded as a brash amateur meddling in matters that were none of his concern. After he left the Admiralty in a storm of notoriety over the Dardanelles fiasco (May 1915), Churchill had to fight tooth and nail in the War Cabinet to prevent the whole programme being scrapped. But enough had been done to prevent this. By the end of June 1915 the navy's anomalous Landships Committee was an inter-service affair and all the talents of the various protagonists of the armoured fighting vehicle were being more and more effectively pooled. These included d'Eyncourt, Swinton, Hetherington, William Tritton, managing director of Foster's, the firm whose big artillery tractors had led to the idea of the Hetherington Big Wheel, Lieutenant W.G. Wilson, a gifted engineer, and Lieutenant Albert Stern, the dynamic secretary of the Landships Committee.

Swinton's persistent dialogue with General Headquarters and with front-line officers produced the basic specifications (9 June 1915) for a combat vehicle suitable for the Western Front. It must have a top speed of at least 4 mph on flat ground, be able to reverse and make sharp turns at top speed. It must be able to climb a 5-feet earth parapet with a one-in-one slope, cross a gap of 8 feet, and have a radius of action of 20 miles. This seems impossibly modest, but was in

Britain's first serious tank prototype, 'Little Willie', goes through its paces, draped with tarpaulins for security purposes.

fact ample for the essential role of tearing open the German trench network and allowing conventional ground forces to take up the running. A crew of ten was suggested, plus an armament of two machine-guns and a light, quick-firing cannon.

These climbing-and-crossing requirements soon ruled out another possibility which had been examined: an armoured version of the little American Killen-Strait tractor, which ran on three tracks and had been tried out as a wire-cutting vehicle. It promised well enough in a strictly limited role but could clearly carry little in the way of armament, and could certainly not cross trenches. It did, however, add to the steadily-growing reserve of experience with tracked vehicles; and on 24 July 1915 a contract was placed with Foster's to develop a larger tracked vehicle which *could* meet the requirements.

Tritton and Wilson, as joint designers, were faced with a major problem: suspension and track. This machine would have to do things that no other vehicle had ever done, and none of the existing suspension and track variants were anything like strong or flexible enough. The Holt system would not do; another version, the American Bullock track, sounded more promising and a lightning order was flashed across the Atlantic for a set. Long before this arrived the first designs for the machine had been finished – it took Tritton and Wilson just three weeks. On 11 August 1915 construction began on the proto-type machine, the Tritton No. 1 or 'Little Willie'. Details of armament – a pom-pom mounted in a circular turret – were sketched in on Little Willie's plans, but this was in every way an experimental machine. While it was still building, Wilson was already roughing out plans for a full-sized fighting variant. This would be rhomboidal or lozenge-shaped in outline and its tracks would run right round the hull – quick, if crude, simplicity, rejecting any attempt at a suspension system. It would stand so high that it could not carry its guns atop the hull: these would have to be mounted in sponsons or blisters jutting out from the sides.

By the end of August 1915 Little Willie was nearly ready for its first powered trials. The Bullock track had arrived from America, and the vehicle crawled for the first time on 8 September. Further tests on the tenth and nineteenth of the same month, however, showed that the Bullock track was as inadequate as that of Holt: Little Willie kept crawling right off its tracks. But Tritton and Wilson rose magnificently to the challenge. In three days they designed, built and tested a new, lightweight track-plate that stood up to all its bench tests. The decisive breakthrough had been made, and even before the virtues of the new track had been proven with extensive tests on Little Willie, Tritton had been ordered to go ahead with building 'Big Willie'.

By the time the new machine underwent its first running tests – 16 January 1916 – conditions of the strictest secrecy had been clamped on the project. It was Swinton who coined the word 'tank' as a suitable cover.

As the moment for the first trial of Big Willie drew near, General Head-quarters in France was given a further push in the right direction by Churchill, who had resigned from the Cabinet in November 1915 and gone to France as an infantry officer. Churchill had kept closely in touch with the tank experiments of 1915 and, as he put it, 'I conceived myself to be the bearer to them [the army] of a good gift'. He wrote a paper (3 December 1915) called *Variants of the Offensive,* which the C.-in-C., Field-Marshal Sir Douglas Haig, read. Haig sent Major Hugh Elles back to England to find out more about the new machines. Elles came back with a favourable report, and as the time drew on for Big Willie's trials in January 1916 the future looked good.

There were in fact two top-secret trials, both carried out at Hatfield Park on a tough assault course which did its best to represent the worst going the Western Front had to offer. The first trial (29 January) was a dress-rehearsal, attended only by the hard-core protagonists of the tank; the second, on 2 February, was witnessed by the 'top brass' and statesmen – including the Minister for Munitions and the Chancellor of the Exchequer. Both trials were successful, and Lord Kitchener himself asked Stern to take charge of the construction in what was clearly an eminently viable project. The initial order, placed on 12 February, was for 100 machines.

Big Willie, or 'Mother' as the prototype came to be known, was hell for the crew. There were eight of them, of which four were needed to drive. The driver and co-ordinating commander sat in front. One man was needed to brake the tracks on each side for steering. The long naval 6-pounder guns poking forward from the sponsons on each side needed a loader and a gunner apiece. Within months, revisions to the armament imposed a sex discrimination. Tanks which retained the 6-pounder guns were called 'Males'; those armed only with machine-guns were 'Females'. Inside the tank (which, of course, had absolutely no suspension) the noise was deafening and the heat appalling. Later, when tanks got their first taste of action, a new hazard was discovered in 'splash'. Enemy missiles hitting the outside would send fiery fragments whizzing

Big Willie or 'Mother', the first of the many, copes with an extremely modest 'trench' during her decisive trials at Hatfield Park in January 1916. The sponson-mounted guns are 6-pounders; the trailing wheels, intended to aid steering, were soon omitted when they were found to be more of a hindrance than a help.

around the crew compartment. And naturally in the early days breakdowns were a fact of life.

Recruitment and training was another problem. To start with, there was no experience, no trained crews passing on their knowledge, and no machines for the novices to learn on. Tank crew members had to be mechanically minded, and it was not a mechanically-minded world – motoring itself was barely twenty years old. There was certainly no rush to volunteer. Swinton, invited to recruit men from the Royal Naval Air Service – an obvious choice because of the RNAS's experience with armoured cars – got no volunteers at all because the men were not prepared to accept the army's lower pay scale by transferring! Despite this and other setbacks, however, Swinton had recruited enough officers and men from every branch of the army (as well as from the civilian motor trade) for training to begin on 24 April 1916. Green as they were, the men did have the advantage of common enthusiasm and hence an embryo *esprit de corps*, although the needs of security had given them the unglamorous name of 'Armoured Car Section of the Motor Machine-Gun Service'.

At this point the demands of the war in France intervened, making a nonsense of the learning and training process and pitchforking the tank on to the battlefield long before it was ready. Fifteen months before, the generals had still been hoping for an orthodox victory. Twelve months before, the obvious dead-

First official picture of the tank on the Western Front, Flers-Courcelette sector of the Somme battlefield, September 1916. This is a Female, armed only with machine-guns. The wire-mesh screen for the crew proved to be a natural snag for German wire and was soon abandoned.

lock in France had prompted the first genuine stirrings of interest in tanks on the part of the generals. Six months before, while the track problem was just being beaten with Little Willie, Loos had been fought. After Loos the Allied strategists sat down to plan for the big summer offensive of 1916, an attack on the Somme sector. But on 21 February 1916 the Germans launched their murderous bid to 'bleed the French army white' at Verdun. The French reserves were strained to the limit and the basis of Allied strategy was shaken. As the terrible weeks went by and the agony of Verdun went on and on, Haig came under pressure to bring forward the British offensive on the Somme, which acquired a new and desperate significance. Haig in turn pestered Swinton to send out as many tanks as possible. No matter that there would be only a handful, and insufficiently trained: the tank must make its debut on the Somme.

Much has been made of this as a classic piece of short-sightedness, frittering away a priceless asset for negligible gain. But as far as the history of the tank is concerned it was really a blessing in disguise, and we can find a modern parallel in, of all things, the American space programme of the 1960s. In January 1967 the Apollo 7 spacecraft burned out on the launch-pad, killing its crew. As a result of the disaster so many fundamental safety measures were incorporated that a similar accident was prevented from occurring in space, and perhaps more than once. Much the same was the case with the early tanks. Suppose wiser councils had prevailed and the tanks had been held back until all the obvious mechanical teething troubles had been ironed out and the crews were thoroughly familiar with their machines. Suppose then that a massed force of tanks had been sent into battle, say in the summer of 1917. It was impossible to simulate battle conditions on the Western Front. The tank crews would still have had to learn their combat experience from scratch. The result could well have been a large-scale mechanized catastrophe, with the tanks suffering losses on a par with those of the infantry on the appalling first day on the Somme, and destroying all the confidence which had been invested in them. The sceptics would have been proved triumphantly right, and quite possibly the future of the tank would have been cut off before it had ever been.

As it was, enough was learned on the Somme – at a very low cost – to prove conclusively that tanks *did* work in combat, that they *could* break through defences, that, where they could operate, they *were* irresistible, and that, in short, the tank clearly had a very definite future indeed.

The tank made its debut in war on 15 September 1916, in the assault by the British 14th Army that opened the second phase of the battle of the Somme. Two companies (C and D) – 49 out of the first batch of 50 which had arrived in France at the end of August – were scattered along a 12-mile stretch of front. Of these only 34 made it to their start-lines, the others breaking down or getting lost in the dark as they moved up. The first tank ever to go into action was D1 (Tank No. 1, D Company), commanded by Lieutenant H. W. Mortimore, which attacked ten minutes before the main assault (05.40 hrs 15 September), cleared a German trench, took a handful of astounded German prisoners, and was shortly afterwards knocked out by two direct shell hits, two of the crew being killed. Other tanks broke down, got themselves bogged or jammed in terrain that was too much for them. Some commanders got disoriented and ended up firing on their own infantry. For all that, it was the tanks – operating alone, or at most in twos and threes – which boosted the infantry to their objectives and added the villages of Courcelette and Flers to the British line on 15 September. A legend was born at Flers, where Lieutenant Stuart Hastie and D17 surged triumphantly down the main street with cheering infantry following. The fall of Flers and Courcelette made a spectacular breach in the German line – but the reserves were not at hand to exploit it, and the Germans had lost none of their skill in rapid counter-attack. The breach was sealed almost as soon as it was made.

RIGHT Sluggish and top-heavy, French
Schneider tanks train on deceptively
level terrain – nothing like the churned-up
chaos of the actual front line of the
Western Front battlefields.

BELOW In the disastrous French summer
offensive of 1917, not even Schneider
tanks fitted with experimental turrets
proved much use.

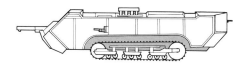

St Chamond.

Apart from the immense benefit of combat experience which could now be passed on to trainee crews, the action of 15 September produced a crop of lessons which were used for the design and production of the second generation of British tanks. The trailing wheels, which had been intended to assist steering, were removed as they had proved more of a hindrance than a help. Other improvements were to take longer: improved armour plate (common-or-garden boiler plate was not good enough protection); a device to prevent the tank from 'ditching', or getting stuck in a trench or shell-hole; and anything which could help a tank across trenches more successfully.

None of the latter refinements had been worked out by March 1917, when the Germans suddenly withdrew to the *Siegfriedstellung* or 'Hindenburg line'. This deliberate retreat to carefully-prepared positions shortened the German front by 25 miles. As the line was designed to be held with the most economical deployment of troops, it also saved the Germans some 13 divisions. Exultantly, the Allies closed up to the line, their morale boosted by traversing unscarred terrain for the first time in over two years. They soon found that their rejoicing was premature.

Tanks were used in the British and French offensive of April 1917: still in insufficient strength, still not fully equipped to tackle battlefield obstacles, but for all that in significantly larger numbers. The plan was for the British to attack on the Arras sector (the northern 'hinge' of the Hindenburg line), while the main French attack would go in across the Chemin des Dames at the other end of the line.

The improved British tank, the Mk IV, was not ready for the Arras-Vimy offensive, the brunt of which fell on the Mk Is and Mk IIs. Weak armour and ditching proved the main drawbacks. The British and Canadian attack of 9–13 April used 70 tanks, committed in much the same way as on the Somme in 1916 and with much the same results. Where the tanks did operate properly they helped the infantry to their objectives in record time, and Vimy Ridge fell.

But the French attack on the Chemin des Dames in the south was a disaster. Manpower losses, the pain of shattered hopes and a sense of utter betrayal drove the French army to widespread mutiny. As far as our story is concerned the French suffered an additional disappointment on the Chemin des Dames: it was the first time that their own tanks saw action, and the results were poor.

The French had good reason to feel bitter about the British as far as tanks were concerned. There had been little or no liaison, and certainly no pooling of experience or suggestion for joint manufacture. The British tank enthusiasts were certainly not to blame: it was all they could do to persuade their own generals and politicians that their ideas were sound. As it happened, the French army had produced a 'Swinton' of its own: Colonel J. E. Estienne, who based his project for an armoured fighting vehicle on the Holt artillery tractors. The French experiments were also born of 1915, the year of frustration, and coincided remarkably (independent as they were) with the British tank programme.

First orders were placed in February 1916: 400 machines from Schneider (the Schneider CA1), followed by another 400 of the larger design produced at St Chamond. The French wanted numbers and economy, not a handful of heavyweights. The Schneider CA1 was half the weight of Britain's Mother (14·6 tons to Mother's 28 tons); the St Chamond weighed 25·3 tons. Both featured a box-like structure atop a comparatively small chassis, with a forward-jutting snout intended to facilitate trench crossing. The Schneider was the first into action, on the Chemin des Dames (16 April 1917), followed by the St Chamond in May. Both were inferior to the British tank in crossing rough ground and trenches. But as they had been ordered in far higher numbers than the British machines, they provided a lot of experience very quickly and encouraged the tank idea to spread (Japan bought a small batch of Schneiders at the close of the war).

1917: Cambrai: a fleeting triumph

British Mk IVs at the time of
Cambrai: (below) wire-crushing;
(bottom) with the 'ditching beam',
which could be hitched to the tracks
and dragged forwards and under to
give a firm foothold and unstick a
'ditched' tank.

RIGHT Crossing a trench (with
'spud' extensions fitted to the tracks
to improve their grip); (below right)
some that did not get back,
recovered, repaired and used by the
Germans.

April 1917 was also the month which saw the first use of tanks in the Middle East. Eight old tanks had been shipped out to join the army facing the Turks in southern Palestine. On 17 April they scored another success for the tank, carrying the infantry to their objectives in the attack on the Turkish positions at Gaza.

With the French Army all but wrecked in the Chemin des Dames offensive, once again the British were called upon to launch a relief attack of their own. The result was 'Third Ypres' or 'Paschendael', a foredoomed, floundering venture in the glutinous swamps of the Ypres salient. At least on the Somme men did not vanish and drown in liquid mud, but the demands on the tanks to play their part were the same. If a carefully hoarded tank force had been committed for the first time at Paschendael, this could well have been the end of the British tank programme. As it was the offensive went on from 31 July to 7 November; and in the latter month Haig finally gave his disgusted tank experts the chance to show what they could do on ground of their own choosing.

The Tank Corps, as it was now known, was headed by Elles who had been promoted to general. He had Lieutenant-Colonel J.F.C. Fuller, the first genius at tank tactics in the field, on his staff. Together they planned a massed tank attack on the Cambrai sector, where the wire lay thick before the German line but the ground was firm and uncratered. This was the first large-scale tank attack in which tanks carried their own artificial aids into battle: ditching beams, to get out when bogged down, and fascines, huge brushwood bundles which tanks could drop into trenches and crawl over. Elles and Fuller also insisted on surprise: no prolonged artillery bombardment to give the game away. This was to be a deliberate, head-on butt at the defences of the Hindenburg line, using weapons and tactics specifically designed to punch straight through.

The battle of Cambrai opened brilliantly on 20 November 1917. Along an entire sector almost six miles wide, tanks flattened the German wire, then ripped lanes in it with grapnels to let the infantry through. As the fascine tanks crossed each successive trench in the Hindenburg line, the first machine across wheeled sharply aside to clear it of German machine-gunners. The unprecedented breakthrough reached up to 4000 yards deep into the German rear areas. But while the church bells rang prematurely in England – the only time in the war – the great opportunity passed. There were no reserves for a full-scale breakthrough and exploitation apart from horsed cavalry, which proved as useless as ever in the face of stiffening German resistance. The Cambrai attack proved, literally, a nine-days' wonder, and the Germans replied with a spirited counter-offensive which left the British with just another costly salient in their front line.

For all that, the Cambrai experiment was a resounding success for the tank, which achieved all and more than had been hoped for the new weapon. The cost was high and offered much food for thought; out of the 324 tanks which went in on 20 November 71 dropped out due to mechanical failure, 43 through ditching and 65 were knocked out by direct hits – a total of 179. But at last an answer to the trench deadlock had been found and proved workable. Cambrai was the logical development from the first experiments on the Somme, and the next step should have been a 1918 Allied offensive which aimed at multiple 'Cambrais' to shatter the German line.

From December 1917, however, the Allies were faced with an appalling prospect. Russia was out of the war and the Germans could transfer thousands of men to the Western Front: all the Allied attacks of the last three and a half years had come to nothing, and now it was their turn to fight for their lives.

Meanwhile, tank development was proceeding apace in the light of lessons learned in 1916–17. A new breed of tank was emerging in Britain and France: light and fast, designed to exploit breakthroughs made by the slower 'heavies'. William Tritton first suggested a 'chaser' tank in December 1916, and this was worked up into the Medium A or Whippet. Only 14 tons, the Whippet could make 8 mph and was armed with four machine-guns, but its awkward design

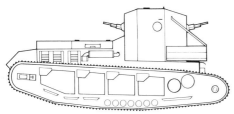

Whippet.

The French move up to mass production with their Renault M-17, a diminutive machine-gun carrier, yet revolutionary in the adoption of a revolving turret.

made life frantically busy for the crew. The driver had to handle not one but *two* engines (for altering speed and direction); the commander had to help the gunner to fire the machine-guns, which poked out of the four sides of a fixed, armoured box, as well as planning his action.

In France the accent was still on producing a lot of lightweights. The unsatisfactory Schneiders and St Chamonds were followed by the Renault M-17, a two-man machine of only 6·7 tons, which could carry either a machine-gun or a 37-mm gun. It was flimsy and a bad trench-crosser (even the Whippet could cross 7 feet, while the M-17 had trouble with 6 feet), but it was a historic tank. It was the first to have a revolving turret, and its high production (the initial order was for 1000 machines) made for a powerful influence on other nations. The United States entered the war in April 1917 and adopted the M-17 for mass production at home. An M-17 captured from the White Russians served as the pattern for Soviet Russia's first tank, the Lenin. Neither the Whippet nor the M-17, however, were ready for large-scale use before the spring of 1918.

The Germans had in the meantime woken up – far too late – to the need for producing tanks of their own. After the Somme an order went out to produce a prototype and the result was the A7 V, very much a panic measure, featuring a towering armoured box on a Holt chassis. The A7 V was a massive 30 tons with an equally massive crew of 18. Main armament was a 57-mm gun poking out of the front armour, two machine-guns on each side and another two at the back. Such a contraption needed three teams of specialists for its crew: infantrymen for the machine-guns, artillerymen for the 57-mm, and mechanics for the two 100-hp engines, making close teamwork nearly impossible due to inter-service rivalry. Maximum speed was never more than 5 mph in ideal conditions and the A7 V proved dangerously top-heavy. Germany's industry could not be adapted to mass production, and only 20 A7 Vs were completed. These, too, were not ready until the spring of 1918.

The 'Ludendorff offensive' which broke upon the Allies on 21 March 1918 concentrated first on the British south of Arras – ironically, on the old Somme

and Cambrai sectors. German superiority was massive: 67 divisions to 33 British, 4,010 light guns to 1,710 British, 2,588 heavy guns to 976 British. The German plan was to saturate all British trench areas with shellfire and send in high-speed waves of 'storm troops', bypassing pockets of resistance, flooding into the rear areas. Specialized infantry and artillery tactics were the key. Tanks were irrelevant – no tank then in existence could have kept pace with the advance. The British, faced with such appalling odds, had dotted their tanks along the line to give as much local support to the infantry as possible – but although they failed to prevent a massive German breakthrough at St Quentin, they gave sterling service. On 22 March, a counter-attack by 25 tanks staved off the Germans at Bapaume and gave the retreating infantry a desperately-needed respite. A brilliant debut by the new Whippets near Serre on the twenty-sixth stopped a threatened German breakthrough and again enabled a gap to be closed in the nick of time. And on 24 April tank fought tank for the first time, when the Germans threw in 13 of their A7 Vs near Villers-Bretonneux.

The British reaction to enemy tank attack was identical to that of the Germans in previous encounters: the infantry panicked and fled. The first British tanks to move against their German opposite numbers were Mark Vs – two Females and a Male. The 57-mm gun of the first German tank sighted drove off the Females, but Lieutenant F. Mitchell's Male took up the running and scored hits. The German tried to take evasive action, ran up a bank and overturned while of the next two A7 Vs on the scene one retreated and the other was deserted by its crew. The retreat of the A7 Vs was followed up by a triumphant charge by seven Whippets, which got in among the German infantry and killed about 400 of them. The Royal Tank Regiment still recalls with pride that one of the victors at Villers-Bretonneux was No. 1 Tank of No. 1 Section, A Company, 1st Battalion.

It was a true omen of what was to come when the German offensive finally ran out of steam in June–July 1918 and the Allies – the British, French and now the Americans – turned again to the offensive. By now the Whippet had been so

A7 V.

German reply: the swarming crew of an A7 V, 1918.

well proven in battle that the Germans had started to develop an improved imitation, the LK II. The best Allied tank was now unquestionably the British Mk V, the first tank to carry an engine specifically designed for an armoured fighting vehicle (the 150-hp Ricardo) and the first British rhomboidal 'heavy' to dispense with gearsmen and leave all the driving to one crew member, vastly improving crew efficiency. The Mk Vs took part in a number of successful 'Cambrais' which preceded the last major single battle of the First World War on the Western Front: Amiens, 8 August 1918.

It was purely due to the mobile firepower and fighting efficiency of the tank that Foch, the Allied Generalissimo, was able to order a major assault with only three weeks' preparation. (The Amiens attack was in fact virtually the only Allied venture which had been brought *forward* by two days instead of being repeatedly postponed.) The attack front east of Amiens spanned 14 miles, and behind it waited 324 fighting tanks to lead the assault, 96 Whippets to exploit the breakthrough, and a reserve and supply force of 184 machines. The result was a resounding success for the Allies, the savaging and collapse of six German divisions – all in all what Ludendorff called the *Schwarze Tag* – the 'Black Day' of the German Army – not merely because of the size of the defeat, but because after it the German soldier's morale was badly shaken and could never be restored. For this the tank was largely responsible.

Amiens has been called 'a second Waterloo'. This would be stretching the bow a little; in 1815 the battle of Waterloo was not followed by three months of desperately hard-fought retreat, with Napoleon's will to resist eroded by socialist upheavals all over France and outbreaks of mutiny. But as far as the tank's history is concerned, the description is accurate enough. Cambrai had been the dress rehearsal; Amiens was the triumphant debut which proved that the tank could win a decisive battle in a day. And from 8 August to 11 November 1918 – from Amiens across the Hindenburg line to Mons in Belgium, where the original German offensive of 1914 had met with its first check – there was no single major engagement in which tanks did not play a crucial role.

ABOVE The scent of final victory: a column of British Mk Vs prepares to assault the Hindenburg line in 1918. The bulky fascines are for dropping into the cavernous German trenches to assist the crossing.

OPPOSITE ABOVE The ignominious debut of the A7 V at Villers-Bretonneux: 'Elfriede' capsized after her brief sniff of action, 24 April 1918, the first tank-v-tank encounter.

OPPOSITE BELOW British lightweights: Whippets moving up, Villers-Bretonneux, 1918.

'Mother' and M-17: Britain and France take the lead

RIGHT AND BELOW 'Mother' type: Mk I Male.

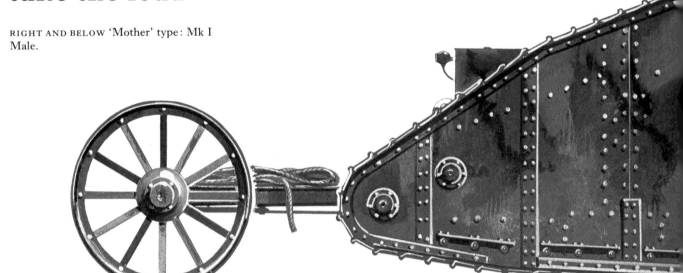

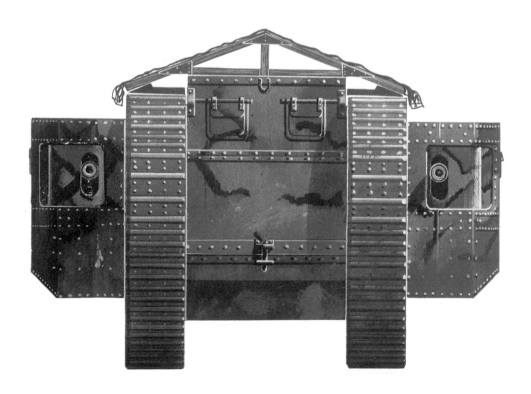

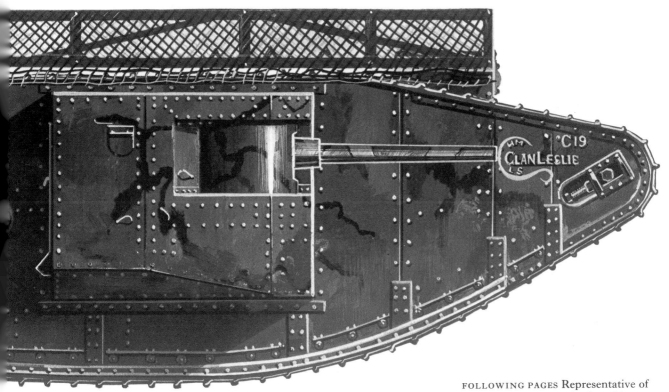

FOLLOWING PAGES Representative of
French tank thinking in the mid 1920s:
the Renault M-24/25, obviously
dominated by the original M-17 design,
trying to improve its obstacle-crossing
performance with raise-and-lower wheels
on the front.

BELOW Renault M-17.

3 Forgotten Lessons

Russia's BT-7:
Christie's dream becomes reality

The First World War ended with Britain and France dominating the world as far as tanks were concerned; no other country could match either their accumulated expertise or numbers of machines. The war also ended with the British on the verge of a total breakthrough in battle tactics. Fuller had already produced his 'Plan 1919' which envisaged a simulated orthodox attack in the centre and deep penetration by massed tanks advancing on each flank. But the 1918 Armistice came before the machines had been produced that alone could make Plan 1919 work. Fuller had wanted tanks capable of at least 20 mph, for rapid penetration to the enemy's rear areas was essential to his plan – but the coming of peace removed the stimulus needed to keep tank design moving. Just as important, it shut off the supply of vast sums of money which had hitherto been available to make the ideas work.

Britain's tank production in the 1920s devolved on the firm of Vickers, which was understandably motivated by the lure of low cost and high export potential rather than the fulfilment of Plan 1919. Despite these weaknesses, Vickers did introduce the rotating turret into British tank design with the Medium II (1922), which went a long way beyond the Medium A, B, C and D designs that succeeded Whippet in 1918. Medium II was a lightweight machine (13·5 tons against Whippet's 14 tons) and could make 18 mph. Its turret gun was a 47 mm and it sprouted six ·303-inch machine-guns, far too many for the crew of five. For all that the Vickers Medium II was the tank on which the British Army experimented with armoured formations in the 1920s.

A whole host of Vickers-inspired tanks boosted experimentation abroad. The Mark C went to Japan in 1926; the light 6-tonner (1928) was exported to Russia and produced there as the T-26A, and in Poland as the 7TP. Germany, banned from possessing tanks by the treaty of Versailles, experimented in secret with the Vickers-originated *Leichte Traktor* on Soviet testing-grounds. The American army also modified the Vickers Medium D, but made no significant improvement. American military thinking in the 1920s was infantry-dominated. The pace and independence of the tank, and the opportunities it offered, had not yet been grasped across the Atlantic.

The same applied to the French, in the 1920s the possessors of the strongest army in Europe. French military thinking was reactionary, obsessed with the pace of infantry – a fatal inhibiting factor when applied to tank design. The Renault M-17, that lightweight machine-gun carrier, was retained until 1930; and the new battle tank developed by the French in the 1920s was a puzzling combination of technical improvements and reactionary thinking.

This was the Char-B. It was intended to be slow-moving (its maximum speed was 17 mph). It was massively armoured (60 mm maximum). It was given the punch of mobile artillery in the form of a short 75-mm gun mounted in the hull and a 47-mm turret gun, plus two machine-guns. It had an economical crew of four with a wildly uneven work-load, for Char-B only had a small, one-man turret. The wretched commander had to fire the 47-mm gun, command and direct his own crew, and co-ordinate his own tank's movements with those of other machines and the accompanying infantry. At 32 tons, Char-B was 4 tons heavier than Mother back in 1916. Char-B's profile did in fact suggest the original rhomboidal tanks with their tracks running right round the hull, but its cross-country performance was vastly superior. This, with its formidable armoured shell, were Char-B's two main virtues.

When it came to producing a successor to the M-17, the French came up with no surprises. The D-1 and D-2 of the early 1930s served as useful test-beds for the new 'light mechanized divisions' – *Division Légère Mécanique*, or DLM. The latter's role was seen mainly as reconnaissance, but it was clear that the old reliance on machine-guns alone was out of date. The lessons learned with D-1 and D-2 resulted in two improved models produced by Renault and Hotchkiss: the R-35 and the H-35. Both featured a 37-mm turret gun and modern-looking,

Major-General J. F. C. Fuller, the brains behind 'Plan 1919' – British founding father of tank strategy.

Char-B1 *bis*, the French heavyweight evolved during the 1920s and 1930s: massively armoured but retaining the inadequate one-man turret, and with the 75-mm armament fixed restrictively in the hull.

but expensive, cast armour hulls and turrets. Their Cletrac steering was a definite improvement: instead of braking a track in order to steer, power was switched from one track to the other by a differential. But both the R-35 and the H-35 were basically the old M-17 writ large; both were as slow as the massive Char-B; both had the inadequate one-man turret; and both were intended to be used like mechanized cavalry.

These French machines clung to the original concept of the light tank as an armoured machine-gun carrier; but this was by no means a blind alley in armoured fighting vehicle development. One lesson of the First World War had been learned, and learned well: gone were the days when the machine-gun could be written off as an overrated weapon. It was accepted that machine-gunners could dominate whole sectors of a battlefield, and the idea of mounting a machine-gun in a tracked armoured vehicle offered the infantry tremendous opportunities.

In Britain these opportunities were explored in freelance fashion during the 1920s. This was completely typical of all previous armoured fighting vehicle experimentation and the causes were the same: high-level disinterest and financial stringency. This time the military master-mind was Major Giffard Martel, his designers were Messrs Carden and Loyd, and production resources were made available by William Morris, the motor car manufacturer. The result was a rash of experimental models, all with similar specifications: about three tons in weight, capable of speeds up to 25 mph, armed with a single forward-pointing machine-gun, with a single or two-man crew usually open to the sky.

Panzer mainstay: the Mk III medium

RIGHT AND FAR RIGHT PzKpfw IIIE.

BELOW The comfort of armoured cover: German troops advance with a PzKpfw III in the last push for Moscow, 1941.

French 'cavalry' tank of the mid 1930s: the Renault R-35, again with a one-man turret to add to the burdens of the commander.

Carden-Loyd produced the most successful carriers and was purchased by Vickers in 1928. The money and resources made available by the takeover enabled steady and rapid progress to the Bren Carrier Mark I of 1935, which was to perform sterling service in the Second World War.

Similar vehicles were eagerly purchased, modified and developed outside Britain: the UE in France, the T-27 in Soviet Russia, the CV-33/35 in Italy, the TK-3 in Poland and the Skoda MU-4 in Czechoslovakia. By the mid 1930s, after an overall development of little more than a decade, the infantry machine-gun carrier had arrived as an armoured fighting vehicle, joining the wheeled armoured car, the light, the medium and the heavy battle tank. All the basic ingredients of Fuller's Plan 1919 were now in existence.

But the theory of how these machines should be used in battle remained desperately muddled during the 1920s and 1930s. Despite all the lessons of 1916–8, it was still widely believed that tanks had no future in modern war – anti-tank guns, mines, and tank traps made tanks a suicidal proposition. Then there was the problem of internal service rivalry between the various arms. 'Cavalry mania' was still very much alive, symbolized by Field-Marshal Sir Douglas Haig's deathless comment in 1925:

'... I am all for using aeroplanes and tanks, but they are only accessories to the man and the horse, and I feel sure that as time goes on you will find just as much use for the horse – the well-bred horse – as you have ever done in the past.'

For their part the infantry pundits argued that infantry must always be the decisive arm in battle and that no conceivable weapon of war could ever change that fact. And they were right: battles will always be won by soldiers defeating their opposite numbers. But instead of treating the new machines as power tools to enable the infantry to do its job faster and more economically, the infantry fanatics criticized armoured fighting vehicles because the infantry could not

Woolly thinking on what tanks were for was only intensified by the misleadingly-dubbed 'tankettes' of Carden-Loyd. This combination has a Mk VI trailer towing a 20-mm anti-tank gun plus crew car, all on tracks. Machine-gun carriers were a boon for the infantry rather than for a separate tank arm, and the best product of the Carden-Loyd stable proved to be the ubiquitous Bren Carrier of the Second World War.

keep pace with them. The idea of the 'infantry tank' was obviously sound: there was never any serious objection to tanks, operating at walking pace, acting as 'can-openers' for infantry in attack. But most military minds could not grasp the limitations of this role, and distrusted the 'all-tank' heretics who pleaded the case for specialized tanks which could exploit and pursue as well as scoring localized breakthroughs.

Artillerymen were equally confused. Although the First World War had proved that the heaviest artillery bombardments could not be relied on to cut holes in barbed wire, let alone puncture enemy defensive systems, the artillery was another arm with a paralysing tradition of prestige. No intelligent general could fail to see the theoretical advantage of putting cannons in tanks and moving packets of fire-power about the battlefield to where they would be most effective – but again the majority opinion recoiled from the notion of an independent tank arm, with its own specialized role to play, working in collaboration with traditional artillery.

In this blur of woolly thinking it was not surprising that terminology became dangerously vague in the 1920s and 1930s. Everything armoured that crawled on tracks, whether armed with cannon or machine-guns, with or without a revolving turret, was called a 'tank'; even the flyweight machine-gun carriers were dubbed 'tankettes'. This passage from Ernest Hemingway's *For Whom The Bell Tolls,* set in the Spanish Civil War of 1936–9, sums it all up:

'It was a cold day and the yellow dust was blowing down the street and Montero had been hit in the left arm and the arm was stiffening. "We have to have a tank," he said. "We must wait for the tank, but we cannot wait." His wound was making him sound petulant.

'Robert Jordan had gone back to look for the tank which Montero said he thought might have stopped behind the apartment building on the corner of the tram-line. It was there all right. But it was not a tank. Spaniards called anything a tank in those days. It was an old armoured car.'

Spaniards were by no means the only people who 'called anything a tank in those days'. But by the outbreak of the Spanish Civil War unforeseen changes had been made to tank theory as well as tank design, and not by the victors of the First World War. In fact the new doctrines had taken root in two nations which had been forced to rebuild their armed forces from virtually nothing since 1918: Soviet Russia and Germany. To both nations the Spanish Civil War was far more than a brushfire war on the periphery of Europe. It was an invaluable testing-ground for new machines and new ideas.

Britain's Valentine:
chronically under-gunned

Massed Valentines train in England.

4 The Coming

of the Panzers

Germany and Soviet Russia were driven into an unnatural but inevitable alignment after 1918. They were the black sheep of the treaty of Versailles – Germany as the arch-villain of the First World War and Soviet Russia because of the excesses of the Bolshevik Revolution. The provisions of Versailles cut Germany down to an army of 100,000 men with no tanks, heavy artillery, warplanes, submarines or heavy capital ships – but no such conditions were laid on Russia. Germany naturally turned to Russia as a proving-ground for secret rearmament; the Russians, for their part, were only too pleased to call on the military expertise of the country which had produced the finest professional army in Europe.

German-Soviet military co-operation began with the granting of concessions (1921) to Krupp and Junkers to set up armaments factories in Russia. This was followed rapidly by the German-Soviet Rapallo Treaty (1922) and the establishment of ammunition factories, a flying school, aircraft engine manufacturing and even a poison gas factory. Finally (1929) a tank training ground was set up at Kazan on the Volga for joint experiments and manoeuvres.

The tanks tested abroad by Germany in the 1920s (in Sweden as well as in the Soviet 'tractor factory') were the LK II of 1918 vintage, the *Leichte Traktor* and the follow-up *Grossetraktor,* the latter being a slow-moving heavyweight which owed much to contemporary Vickers designs. Meanwhile the Russians continued to buy specimens of the newest foreign designs, including the lighter,

PREVIOUS PAGES A trio of PzKpfw Is, the first Panzers, rattles out of a smokescreen during manoeuvres in 1936.

BELOW Rejected in its native United States but adopted enthusiastically by the Russians: the prototype Christie Cruiser with its revolutionary wheels-or-track drive, which boosted tank cross-country speeds to new records.

faster Carden-Loyds. Under the regime of Klimenti Voroshilov, Soviet Army Commissar, Russian designers swung away from traditional slow-paced infantry tanks. The Russian ideal was a tank which combined high speed across country with turret gun and machine-gun armament: a fast gun-platform. Like the French in 1916–7, they also wanted designs which lent themselves to mass production. All this was of the highest value to the German observers – but Hitler's accession to power as Chancellor in January 1933 and the winding-up of the Kazan scheme came just too early for the Germans to see which way Russian tank design was heading by the mid 1930s: enthusiastic adoption of the revolutionary tank design of the American J. Walter Christie.

Christie was an extraordinary designer, a loner with a lot of the maverick in his make-up, who above all else refused to be dominated by current trends. Starting with several tracked artillery carriers towards the close of the First World War, he fastened upon one of the tank's greatest weaknesses: what happened to its tracks in doing its job. In 1919 he came up with a design for a tank which could run at the same speed forward or in reverse, on tracks or on wheels. Large diameter wheels and wide tracks were invariable design features of all Christie variants. By 1928 he had found the answer to the wheel-cum-track drive and was persevering with the demands of high-speed cross-country performance. His M-1931 design shattered all previous tank speed records – the 30 mph barrier was broken at last – and was promptly purchased by Russia. The result, three years later, was the production-line turnout of Russian *Bystrokhodnye* ('fast') tanks, all with the prefix 'BT' and with the distinctive Christie wheels and track features.

But by the time the first BT tanks entered service with the Red Army the Germans had already decided to go ahead with a line of tanks which owed more to Carden-Loyd than it did to Christie.

The deadly and ingenious use of *Panzertruppen* – armoured troops – by the German army in the Second World War almost totally obscures the fact that right down to 1939 the German army contained quite as many reactionaries as any other army in the world – men who thoroughly distrusted mechanization in general and the tank in particular, and did everything they could to block tank development. Detractors of Adolf Hitler also tend to ignore the fact that his vision and encouragement were decisive factors in the development of the legendary Panzer divisions.

Undoubtedly the greatest name in 'Panzer lore' is that of Heinz Guderian, a brilliant field commander as well as a clear-brained planner and administrator. Guderian was no mechanic: his First World War service had been with the *Jägers*, the light infantry. But in the early 1920s he was plunged willy-nilly into the technical problems of mechanization. If the 100,000-man German army was to be fully efficient, it must obviously make more use of motorized troops. All previous experience with motorized troops had to be rationalized and Guderian was one of the officers assigned to the job. He started by pleading his total lack of qualifications, but when his protests were overruled he buckled down to the task and read voraciously on everything to do with the subject.

This reading introduced him to the novel theories of the British 'prophets without honour in their own country' – Fuller and the new rising star, Captain Basil Liddell Hart. Guderian soon made contact with the other revolutionaries in the German army who were also looking to the future – Colonel von Reichenau, Major von Thoma, Colonel Lutz. They formed a vociferous but heartily distrusted nucleus of military opinion that held that armoured fighting vehicles should not be restricted to infantry co-operation, or scattered along the front line, weak everywhere, strong nowhere. Tanks should be massed not only in brigades but in divisions – better still, in corps – and flung *en masse* against the weakest sector of the enemy front.

Prophet without honour: Basil Liddell Hart, whose theories on tank strategy bore no fruit in Britain but were avidly read and adopted by the German Panzer pioneers.

The Panzer forces which Guderian and his colleagues advocated were not to be 'all-tank' units. Just as Napoleon had revolutionized the military breakdown by introducing army corps, each with its balanced complement of horse, foot and guns, the new Panzer units were seen as balanced teams of complementary arms: motor-cycles with machine-guns, armoured cars for reconnaissance, light tanks, medium tanks, self-propelled artillery and motorized infantry. Until Hitler became chief of state this programme was officially regarded as the rankest heresy in official army circles, as the following selection of *obiter dicta*, recorded with irony in Guderian's memoirs, clearly shows:

'To hell with combat! They're supposed to carry flour!' (Request for transport vehicles for motorized units, 1924.)

'You're too impetuous. Believe me, neither of us will ever see German tanks in operation in our lifetime.' (General Otto von Stülpnagel, Inspector of Motorized Troops, spring 1931.)

'You should realize that all technicians are liars.' (General Freiherr von Fritsch, C.-in-C. of the Army, 1933.)

'No, no, I don't want to have anything to do with you people. You move too fast for me.' (General Ludwig Beck, Army Chief of the General Staff, 'the finest brain in the army', 1933.)

What mattered, however, were the results shown on manoeuvres when Guderian was allowed to test his new ideas with dummy tanks: unprecedented success. And in 1933 the new Chancellor, Hitler, watched a thirty-minute demonstration by Guderian's men and burst out: 'That's what I need! That's what I want to have!'

The machines Hitler watched in that fateful demonstration were very different from the sluggish heavyweights experimented with in the 1920s. The last of these, a derivation of the *Grossetraktor*, had been the *Panzerkampfwagen* V ('armoured battle vehicle' or PzKpfw V for short): massive armour of 70 mm thickness, a crew of six, one 75-mm turret gun and two machine-guns. But this lumpish monster weighed 35 tons (against the 32 tons of France's Char-B). Far more practical for the short-term need of a massed-produced lightweight tank for training was a Carden-Loyd derivative produced by Krupp. This was eventually designated PzKpfw I: 5·5 tons in weight with a crew of two, wafer-thin armour of 12 mm, a turret carrying nothing more than two machine-guns and a speed of 22 mph. It was a makeshift contrivance and it looked like one, with its wheels linked by coupling-rods. But a platoon of these midgets performed so impressively for Hitler that they secured his deep interest in armoured formations, and PzKpfw I went into mass production in 1934. It was followed by the PzKpfw II (with a 20-mm cannon in the turret) and plans raced ahead for the second generation of medium tanks: the PzKpfw III with a 37 mm gun and the PzKpfw IV with a 75-mm gun.

In March 1935 Hitler rejected the '*diktat*' of Versailles, announced the re-introduction of conscription, and officially revealed the existence of the new *Luftwaffe,* the German air force. And on 15 October the first three Panzer divisions were formed. Even then, Germany's 'cavalry mentality' was strong enough to insist on the formation of three so-called 'light divisions' – paper tigers which, after testing in combat, were eventually up-graded into Panzer divisions. At this time, too, the first motorized divisions were formed – four of them.

BELOW Deprived of tanks by the treaty of Versailles, the German army of the 1920s and early 1930s was forced to train with dummies mounted on trucks.

BOTTOM Learning infantry–armour co-operation – PzKpfw I with infantrymen on manoeuvres.

BELOW Panzer parade: PzKpfw Is of the first Panzer divisions are reviewed on Party Day in September 1936 by the armed forces commanders, Fritsch, Blomberg and Grand-Admiral Raeder.
BOTTOM Panzer punch: a PzKpfw I copes easily with a brick wall during a public demonstration.

1933: 'That's what I need! That's what I want to have!' –Hitler

RIGHT PzKpfw II, with 20-mm cannon, hurling its three-man crew about mercilessly on a cross-country exercise.

BELOW A windfall for the *Wehrmacht*, the excellent Czechoslovak Skoda tanks, taken over *en masse* after Munich by courtesy of Britain and France, gave Germany three new Panzer divisions. This is a 38t.

PzKpfw I.

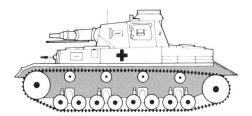

PzKpfw IVA.

Panzer mastermind Guderian coping with deskwork in the summer of 1939, weeks before leading his units into battle in Poland.

The first Panzer divisions were made up as follows. The cutting edge was the Panzer brigade of 561 tanks, supplemented by a motorized infantry brigade, an anti-tank battalion, an armoured reconnaissance battalion made up of motor-cycle and armoured car companies, an artillery regiment, a signals battalion and a light engineer company. Panzer troops did not spring into existence fully armed and efficient: the machines were not ready, there was far too much insistence upon infantry support, and the whole problem of supplying a mobile column of armoured vehicles was a closed book. All this took time to put right. But the basic decision to start early gave Germany the most superior tank arm in the western world by 1939–40, the first ten months of the Second World War, in which Germany won the greatest sequence of victories in her history.

These machines – PzKpfw II, III and IV – set new standards in combined efficiency. Large turrets freed the commander from the distraction of aiming and firing the gun. Radio communications and field signalling were given top priority. Thickness of armour was emphatically not a characteristic of the early Panzers (Mk IV A's thickness was only 20 mm). Nor was speed: the little Mk II could make over 30 mph but Mks III and IV had to be content with 20 mph and 22 mph respectively. But the first Panzers were superb compromises aimed at mass production, mixed fire-power, and maximum fighting efficiency. The 'short', low-velocity 75-mm gun carried by the Mk IV could fire either anti-tank solid shot or high explosive shell.

Before German tank production had had the time to get into high gear, the German take-over of Czechoslovakia gave the Panzer arm 469 of the excellent Skoda 35t. The latter was one of the best Vickers refinements produced in any country, and Germany acquired sufficient to equip three new Panzer divisions.

The combat experience provided by the Spanish Civil War was limited to a handful of early Panzers – far too few to try out the new theory of assault in mass. It was learned, however, that it was no longer possible for lone tanks to raise havoc behind or in front of the enemy lines: modern fire-power was too intense. At least Guderian's revulsion from dispersion of armour was confirmed. Another promising innovation was air-ground co-operation. This was the period when the new *Luftwaffe* was also flexing its muscles, and one of the air force's best assets was the pinpoint accuracy of its dive-bombers.

Meanwhile tank design outside Russia and Germany floundered along in the wake of these incredible new advances.

5 The Triumph of the Panzers

As the 1930s drew to a close it was already obvious that the treaty of Versailles and the League of Nations had failed in their attempt to put the final seal on 'the war to end all wars'. And the Franco-British tank supremacy, like the entire Allied victory of 1918, had been frittered away by lethargy, the dead hand of military tradition, and peacetime economy.

The basic trends in tank development between the wars are not only easy to define with the gift of hindsight: they were recognized at the time by men of vision and energy whose arguments were ignored in favour of the soft option and personal rivalry and prejudice.

The First World War had established the armoured car, the slow but massive infantry tank and the faster light tank. To these, in the 1920s and 1930s, were added the light machine-gun carrier for the infantry plus an entirely new breed of tank: the medium or cruiser, raised to unheard-of performances by Christie's innovations.

Experiments in Britain and Germany had proved conclusively that balanced forces of tanks and motorized infantry could achieve startling results. But whereas the Germans went ahead and produced the first Panzer divisions, the British produced one armoured brigade and had only begun on their first armoured division by 1939.

Having mastered basic armoured manoeuvres with the PzKpfw I and II, and received the unexpected bonus of the Czech Skoda 35ts, the Germans were pressing ahead with the production of their new mediums: PzKpfw III and IV.

PREVIOUS PAGES PzKpfw IIIJ, with long 50-mm gun, during the Stalingrad–Caucasus campaign of 1942, the last year of Mk III production.

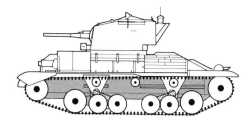

Cruiser A-9.

The British, however, had turned about and gone right back to the days of the First World War. On the advice of General Elles, of Cambrai fame, they were producing infantry tanks: the Infantry Mark I, with 65 mm of armour, a London bus engine giving a top speed of 8 mph, and the derisory armament of a single ·303-inch machine-gun. (The Infantry Mk II 'Matilda' had a 40-mm 2-pounder gun.)

The heirs of the Vickers medium tanks which had set so many countries' notions of tank development in progress were unsatisfactory contraptions of a different sort. They were Carden-designed caricatures of the Christie cruiser, the A-9 and A-10, angular, flimsy, prone to breaking down and shedding their tracks with maddening abandon. The British light tanks were scaled-up versions of the Carden machine-gun carriers, typified by the Vickers Light Mk VI. This could make 29 mph on good going – far too slow for a light tank – and was armed with two machine-guns. Germany's PzKpfw II had a 20-mm cannon, over double the armour thickness (30 mm against 14 mm) and a top speed of 35 mph.

In France the main heavy battle tank was still the Char-B; the new SOMUA S-35 was also entering service. This was a hybrid cross between Char-B and the light R-35s and H-35s. It had a speed of 25 mph, 55 mm of armour, and a 47-mm gun – but it also had the endemic French weakness of a style-cramping one-man turret. Like Britain, France was woefully late with her decision to create motorized and armoured formations and by 1940 the first *divisions cuirassées* were still not operational.

LEFT Britain's first tank brigade, with Vickers Medium Mk Is, manoeuvres on Salisbury Plain in 1931.

ABOVE An elephant with a peashooter: the absurd British 'Infantry Mark I' with its single ·303-inch machine-gun.

59

1935-1940: the first Russian heavies

RIGHT The huge three-turreted T-35.

LEFT The Vickers-originated, Russian-built T-28.

RIGHT The first modern Russian 'heavy', the KV-I, was just entering service with the Red Army when the Germans invaded in June 1941.

RIGHT A rattletrap lightweight: Britain's
Vickers Light Mk VI.

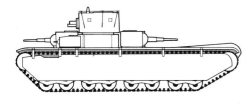

T-35.

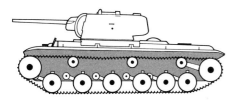

KV-I.

The vast mass of the Soviet armed forces had had to endure the traumatic
frontal lobotomy carried out on it by Stalin in the great officer purges of 1937–8.
These purges brutally achieved the aim of carving out any spirit of initiative and
independent thinking within the Red Army. But although Stalin reduced the
Soviet army to a zombie, it was still a colossal zombie and its tank force continued to expand. By 1941, the year of the German invasion, Soviet tanks outnumbered the German Panzer force four times over – 21,000 armoured fighting
vehicles in all.

Yet the Russians, like the British, had not shaken off the need to dabble in
antiquated designs. The Red Army's BT series had enhanced the Christie
format with excellent results – but in weird contrast to the BTs there was the
grotesque T-35, a land ironclad fit to gladden the heart of H. G. Wells. T-35 had
a crew of ten and a dreadnought battleship-like main armament of *three* turrets:
two 45 mm and a 76 mm. Surprisingly, T-35 could make 18 mph in spite of its
45 tons. But its 30 mm of armour made it easy meat for much smaller tanks. In
addition to this unpractical super-heavy the Russians had also become side-
tracked by inferior but easy-to-produce makeweights like the Vickers-inspired
T-26 and T-28. By 1939, however (and as events proved just in time to avoid
total disaster in 1941), the inherent soundness of the Christie format had
reasserted itself. Mikhail Ilyich Koshkin, master-designer of the BT series,
had completed his outline for the legendary 27-ton T-34 medium tank; and a
much sounder Soviet heavy was being planned in the 46-ton Klementi Voroshilov I (KV-I).

As far as armoured opposition was concerned, the Polish campaign of 1–28
September 1939 (the latter date being the day Warsaw surrendered) was the
easiest the German army ever had to fight in the Second World War. To stand
up to seven Panzer divisions, four motorized divisions and four light divisions,
the Poles only had one light armoured brigade, armed with the seven-year-old
Vickers variant, the 7 TP, and the TK-3 light carrier. For all that, the new
Panzer force had some frightening moments. Guderian himself had to intervene
to stop his forces from retreating in the face of a Polish *cavalry* attack; all
mobile units had to learn the trick of coping with roadblocks and anti-tank guns,
and armour-infantry co-operation could only be painfully learned. Infantry
commanders grumbled at being left to do all the hard fighting while the Panzers
dashed ahead; Panzer commanders grumbled at being tied down by requests
for tanks to help the infantry grind down surrounded pockets of enemy infantry.

France's SOMUA S-35, the last logical development from the basic tank concepts of 1917 that inhibited French tank development throughout the 1920s and 1930s.

But in general the Polish campaign was a mine of priceless experience. Guderian and his colleagues found that by riding in command vehicles, as far forward as they could get without actually running down the enemy's throat, an armour commander could seize upon a fleeting opportunity and make decisive advance after advance.

The Norwegian campaign (7 April–10 June 1940) was the preserve of the infantry. The bulk of the German armour was needed for the decisive campaign in the Low Countries and France, which was opened once it was clear that victory in Norway was assured. A handful of light tanks was sent to Norway where they operated in the tank's most primitive role: providing cover and support for infantry attacks.

The campaign in the west (10 May–25 June 1940) was the first real test for the Panzers. The ten Panzer divisions (total tank strength 2690 with 800 in reserve in Germany) were outnumbered by the French alone in overall numbers – counting reserve and training machines, the French could have fielded 3330 tanks. The British contributed another 310 tanks, 100 of them infantry tanks. But it was not a question of numbers. The Allies were weak everywhere, strong nowhere. The Germans peeled off three Panzer divisions to operate in Belgium and Holland and flung the remaining seven against the hinge of the Allied line at Sedan. A special new unit was devised for this: the *Panzergruppe*, a concentration for which the Allied plans were totally unprepared.

In the first phase of the campaign (10–24 May) the *Panzergruppe* punched through the Allied line, romped westward to the Channel (brushing off ineffective Allied counter-attacks as they went), turned north-eastwards along the Channel coast and penned in the British, French and Belgian forces in the Dunkirk pocket. The German armour was deliberately withheld from the attempts to drive the Allies into the sea at Dunkirk; the final battle had still to be fought against the French. This triumphant opening stage had many sobering features. Textbook rules and cautious orders from the top were ignored by the handful to exploit the panic in the Allied centre. Erwin Rommel, commanding the 7th Panzer Division, ordered his tanks to fire salvoes to the left and right while on the move to add to the demoralization of the crumbling French. Ordered not to advance further, but permitted to 'reconnoitre in force', Guderian 'reconnoitred in force' with three Panzer divisions – and reached the Channel within a week of the crossing of the Meuse. A clumsy Franco-British attempt to shut off the 'Panzer corridor' on 21 May by attacking south of Arras was well handled by Rommel. The 37-mm German anti-tank guns proved completely ineffective against the thick armour of the British Matilda infantry tanks and 88-mm anti-aircraft guns, firing in flat trajectory, were pressed into service as an emergency measure. This was the first effective use of this devastating weapon in tank warfare. The French Char-B posed similar problems, but it was easy to outflank and the vertical cliffs of its side armour could be more easily pierced by shellfire.

Panzer debut: a PzKpfw I by the Brahe river in Poland, September 1939.

The thrust to the Channel and its sequel at Dunkirk reduced the Allied opposition by one-third. The new French commander, General Weygand, had 71 divisions with which to face 143 German divisions and to hold the line of the Somme and Aisne rivers. Despite his age (he was seventy-three) Weygand was one of the most imaginative commanders of the Second World War – a fact which is generally ignored because of the debacle of 1940, for which he was not initially responsible. Weygand was no timid fossil from a bygone age: he knew precisely how the Panzer menace should be handled. The attenuated French line must bunch itself into a hedgehog defence, creating gaps which would invite Panzer penetration. The enemy tanks must be lured into the fire of prepared gun positions and the deadly embrace of minefields. Infiltration must be promptly counter-attacked – a bridgehead won by a handful of men today could be held by a brigade tomorrow and a division the day after. Thus Weygand, instead of being branded as the general who lost the battle of France (that honour should be reserved for his lethargic predecessor, Gamelin) should be remembered as an innovator of the calibre of Guderian himself. Guderian perfected the armoured offensive: it was Weygand who discovered the formula for dealing with armoured offensives.

The trouble was that Weygand took up an impossible task. There were no prepared minefields, the bulk of the French armour had already been frittered away, and above all the Germans gave him no time. Weygand took over on 21 May; the Dunkirk evacuation began on the twenty-sixth and ended on 4 June; the following day the German forces, regrouped into three *Panzergruppen*, fell on the French line.

For the first 48 hours the French defences held, and held well. The Germans had never met resistance like it. They were losing tanks at an unprecedented rate – one Panzer battalion had nine tanks knocked out within minutes. It was a shock to find French units maintaining an all-round defence and refusing to panic once the Panzers had bypassed them. But it could not last. The first German punctures were made on the sixth, with Rommel's 7th Panzer once again breaking out into open country and setting a scorching pace of advance. (Between 16–17 May he had made history by advancing 50 miles in 24 hours, through the night; on 12 June his 88 mm guns were duelling with a British warship at St Valery, another 'first' for an armoured division; on 17 June the 7th Panzer broke all records by advancing 150 miles in a single day.)

When Cherbourg surrendered to Rommel on 19 June 1940, it was a resounding finale to one Panzer division's epic campaign. Since 10 May, the 7th Panzer had captured five admirals (one of them the French C.-in-C. North), a corps commander, four divisional commanders with their staffs, 341 guns (64 of them anti-tank guns) and 458 tanks and armoured cars. The smaller fry was too numerous to count: 3000–5000 trucks, 1500–2000 cars, 1500–2000 wagons, 300–400 buses, and 300–400 motorcycles. Nor was this all. The anti-aircraft guns of the division shot down 52 aircraft and destroyed 12 more on the ground; 15 other aircraft were captured by the division. As for Allied prisoners taken by 7th Panzer, it had never been possible to stop and count them – it was as much as the Germans could do to keep the hordes of surrendering soldiers out of the way of the Panzers and direct them to the rear. But all in all the Panzer units were credited with 97,468 prisoners.

The cost for the 7th Panzer Division was tiny: 672 officers and men killed, 1,646 wounded and 266 missing; three PzKpfw I, five PzKpfw II, 26 PzKpfw III and eight PzKpfw IV tanks destroyed. Compared to the First World War bloodbaths, this was a ludicrously small price for one division to pay, with Holland, Belgium and France knocked out and 135 Allied divisions swept from the board.

But despite the superb performance of the Panzer divisions, the German army had not enjoyed a bloodless walk-over. After the end of hostilities on 25

1940: Panzer breakthrough at Sedan

TOP PzKpfw IVs roll down to the Meuse for Guderian's decisive breakthrough at Sedan (13 May) that ripped the Allied front wide open.

LEFT PzKpfw IIs cross a pontoon bridge over a French canal.

BELOW Rommel's 7th Panzer Division in full cry – a picture taken by Rommel himself. The tank nearest the camera is a 38t.

Facing up to the shock appearance of the T-34

One of the most historic pictures of the Second World War; shaken Germans examine three T-34s which have been bogged down and abandoned by their inexperienced crews, summer 1941.

June the German High Command (*Oberkommando der Wehrmacht,* or OKW) put the total German casualty list at 27,074 killed, 111,034 wounded and 18,384 missing – and as all German prisoners taken during the campaign had been handed over, 'missing' mostly meant dead.

There was another, more ominous side to the casualty figures. In the three weeks between the opening of the offensive and Dunkirk, 135 Allied divisions each accounted for 450 Germans killed and wounded daily. In the fortnight under Weygand's command, 4–18 June (when organized resistance can be said to have ended), 71 Allied divisions sent the daily toll rocketing to 1,343 German casualties per division – three times the previous amount, and proof that the now dreaded Panzer divisions were by no means invincible *when met on the right ground with the right tactics.*

In June 1940 the reverse seemed the case – but it soon became apparent that all the heady victories had built a house without a roof. The war did not end. Britain fought on – the German military machine had never seriously considered the possibility that Britain would have to be invaded and conquered too. The 'Sea Lion' invasion plan was prepared with amazing speed and drawn up in 'Führer Directive No. 16' which was signed by Hitler on 16 July. The German army planners had one serious problem: getting tanks into the assault wave and onto the beaches as quickly as possible to support the troops and help them break out of their beach-heads. A solution was tested and found to work: submarine tanks. PzKpfw IIIs and IVs were totally sealed and long hoses, attached to floating buoys, fitted to their exhaust pipes. Tests at Putlos (Holstein) showed that such machines, deposited on a gently-sloping sea bed, could crawl inshore under their own power and emerge on the beach ready to throw off their waterproofing and go straight into action. One obvious drawback was that they could only be used where the sea bed was firm and did not shelve too steeply, which limited the choice of invasion beaches; but when the *Luftwaffe* failed to win total air supremacy over the Channel in the battle of Britain and 'Sea Lion' was postponed indefinitely, this problem became an academic one. Hitler had already ordered advance planning to begin for the invasion of Soviet Russia – but events in southern Europe and the Mediterranean opened up a whole new theatre of war in the autumn of 1940, one in which tanks were forced to operate in conditions varying from the nightmarish to the ideal.

What were the main tank lessons and developments as the autumn of 1940 approached?

For the moment, the Germans were content to put all their eggs in one basket and continue production of the PzKpfw III and IV. German tank production was still comparatively low – hardly more than 1000 machines in 1940. Hitler, obsessed with forming more Panzer divisions, wanted to boost tank production to 1000 units per month, but was talked out of it on practical grounds by the army Ordnance Office. He also wanted to up-gun the PzKpfw III with a high-velocity gun of bigger calibre, the 50-mm L60, but he was again opposed by the Ordnance Office (this time behind his back), who opted for the short-barrelled 50-mm L42. (See Appendix I.) Meanwhile, Panzer production was assisted by the Skoda contribution. From the Czech 35t, German designers produced the 38t, improving its performance by giving it a Christie-type suspension. In addition there were scores of captured French Char-B, H-35 and -39, and R-35 tank hulls which could be used to build a cheap park of armoured self-propelled guns.

One glaring lesson taught by the campaigns in Poland and the west was the need to keep the infantry complements of the Panzer divisions in the closest touch with the armour, and as a result the production of tracked personnel carriers was stepped up. Hitler's demand for double the number of Panzer and motorized infantry divisions put a terrific strain on German industry and could only be met in two ways: by cannibalizing the light divisions which had proved ineffective anyway, and by halving the armoured complement of each Panzer division to make the number of tanks available go further. This meant dropping the number of PzKpfw IIIs and IVs per division to a strength of 150–200 machines. In the short term, this lightening of the Panzers' punch would be more than compensated for by combat experience and tactical skill – but in any long-term struggle with an enemy of sufficient resilience this advantage must be cancelled out by the enemy learning the tricks of the trade too.

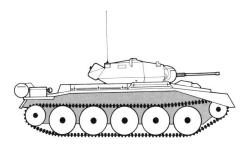

Crusader I.

The best British heavy tank in 1940 and 1941 was the Matilda, the slow Infantry Mk II with its massive armoured shell. As far as cruiser tanks were concerned the British already had A-9 and A-10; with the A-13, blooded in France in 1940, they adopted the Christie suspension at last. A-13 looked very like the Czech-German 38t, although it sacrificed armour for speed – 30 mph against the 38t's 21 mph, but only 14 mm of armour against the 38t's 21 mm. However, A-13 was a transitional machine: its successor, the Crusader, although rushed into action prematurely in 1941 (the fate of many a promising tank design in the Second World War) represented a long step forward from the cranky A-9s and A-10s.

Another promising British tank was nearing completion in autumn 1940: the Valentine, a Vickers design. This was intended to combine the power and strength of the infantry tank with the virtues of the cruiser. Like Matilda, low speed (15 mph maximum) was its biggest drawback, although armour thickness (65 mm) was not sacrificed. At the other end of the scale, no better British light tank than the Vickers Light Mk VI had emerged.

Dunkirk did terrible things to Britain's tank prospects. The British Expeditionary Force left all its machines and guns behind, which meant that development and experimentation with the newer designs had to come second to keeping the older designs in production in order to re-equip the army. An obvious result was the retention of the 2-pounder (40 mm) gun as main tank armament when the PzKpfw IIIs were moving on to 50 mm guns. There were not enough of the scheduled 6-pounder (57 mm) guns to go round; their anti-tank version had priority over the tank turret-gun version, with the result that the up-gunning of British tanks was set back by nearly two years.

In the short term, this did not matter because the first enemy tanks encountered by British armour after Dunkirk were those of Italy in the western desert. Italy's attempt to come up with a modern tank had produced nothing better than the M-11/39, of obvious Vickers parentage. It was slow (20 mph) lightly armoured (29 mm) and weak in main armament (37 mm gun) and its successor, the M-13/40, was not much of an improvement (20 mph in ideal going, 40 mm maximum armour, 47-mm gun). The light Italian weapon carrier the CV-35, normally referred to by the British as a 'light tank', had few if any advantages over the British Bren-gun carrier – certainly not in its machine-guns, the Italian army being the worst equipped of all the major belligerent powers in this weapon.

The opening phase of the North African campaign was momentous, not merely opening up a new theatre of war but eventually siphoning off vital reserves of men and machines from the main war effort of the German-Italian Axis. Italy invaded Egypt from Libya on 13 September 1940, advanced some 30 miles to Sidi Barrani and stopped. On 9 December General Wavell unleashed the tiny mechanized Western Desert Force against the Italians at Sidi Barrani, beginning a runaway advance that threw the Italians not only out of Egypt but out of eastern Libya (Cyrenaica) as well. This phase of the campaign ended at Beda Fomm on 5 February 1941 when those British tanks able to stand the pace of the advance, ambushed the retreating floods of Italians. The score of prisoners at

T-34 and Sherman:
the two Allied workhorses

LEFT AND RIGHT T-34.

CRICKLADE

257

Beda Fomm was reckoned at 25,000, but right from the start – as with the Germans in France – it had been virtually impossible to count heads. One British officer had summed it up on the first day of the offensive by estimating the count of prisoners as 'about five acres of officers and two hundred acres of other ranks'.

The pattern of the North African campaign had been set. The British had proved that tiny armoured forces could take off into the open desert and raise havoc by appearing on the enemy's flank and rear. Unfortunately, they were rapidly given a daunting taste of their own medicine. Hitler, forced to consider the possibility that the British might well keep going and take Tripoli itself, authorized the despatch of a small German armoured force to defend the Libyan capital for his useless ally. When complete this force would consist of the 15th Panzer Division and the 5th Light Division, scheduled to be up-graded as the 21st Panzer Division. Rommel, by far the most successful commander of an individual Panzer division in France, was given the command of this embryo Panzer corps – the *Deutsches Afrika Korps,* or DAK. He was sent

ABOVE The Panzers come to North Africa. PzKpfw IIs in Tripolitania, February 1941, in the early days when sun helmets were still worn by the *Afrika Korps*.

RIGHT Britain's first desert offensive, December 1940: a Matilda rumbles ponderously past smashed Italian gun positions at Sidi Barrani.

out to Tripoli in February 1941 with purely defensive orders and the vague promise that enough reinforcements might be sent out to launch a limited offensive to recover Benghazi in May.

The British were meanwhile pulling desert forces out of the line to form a new expeditionary force to send to the aid of the Greeks. What forces remained were tired and badly deployed. Rommel saw at once that all the sting had gone out of his new opponents and at the end of March 1941 began to bounce the British outposts out of their forward positions. Encouraged by swift British withdrawals, he advanced flat out into Cyrenaica in a three-pronged attack which threw the British back into Egypt. An improvised force, however, manned the former Italian defences of Tobruk and held out behind Rommel's lines. Before he accepted that he would have to mount a formal attack on the place, Rommel sacrificed several experienced Panzer crews in ill-considered attacks against well-sited gun positions and minefields.

Throughout May 1941 the hapless Wavell was under constant pressure from Churchill to attack Rommel. This he could not do. The Greek expedition had

Panther and Firefly:
two answers to enemy superiority

PzKpfw Panther V.

Sherman Firefly.

T269399

been a fiasco resulting in a second Dunkirk, the loss of Greece and Crete, and all the tanks sent there from the desert. The mountains and passes of Greece were the complete opposite of ideal tank terrain, yet the Panzer crews showed energy and flair. They used the firm beds of streams, the ballasted beds of railway lines – even, on one occasion, a railway tunnel – in their energetic hooks at the British flanks.

The British tried to make up the deficit with an emergency tank transfusion, 295 machines being rushed through the Mediterranean in the 'Tiger Convoy' (6–12 May). Churchill, eager to see his 'Tiger Cubs' in action, refused to listen to Wavell's lists of appalling mechanical defects among the new arrivals. 'Battleaxe', the assault on Rommel's frontier defences, went in on 15 June and was a total failure. Dug-in 88-mm guns shattered the armour of the Matildas, while well-judged German flank attacks kept the British off balance and eventually hustled them back to their start lines. It was a resounding victory for Rommel, and an economical one: about 100 out of 180 Tiger Cubs were destroyed for the cost of 12 Panzers.

The following week – 22 June 1941 – the German invasion of Soviet Russia, 'Barbarossa', was launched. The assault was carried by three German army groups – North, Centre and South, aimed at Leningrad, Moscow and Kiev respectively, with a front-line strength of 17 Panzer divisions and 11 motorized divisions deployed in four *Panzergruppen*: 3090 tanks. But only 439 of them were PzKpfw IVs, and Germany's Panzer experts such as Guderian had uncomfortable suspicions that the Red Army had some nasty surprises to spring. Russians inspecting German tank factories under the terms of the

Rommel's trump: the 88-mm AA gun in its anti-tank role, with a PzKpfw IV in attendance. The '88' was the only German gun capable of killing the heavy British Matilda in the first year of the desert war.

Nazi-Soviet Non-Aggression Pact of August 1939 had flatly refused to believe that the PzKpfw IV was the heaviest German tank, accusing the Germans of concealing the newest models. The Panzer experts were far from happy about Soviet tank potential, but Hitler refused to listen.

The formidable demands made on the Panzer divisions by the 'Barbarossa' plan were many: unheard-of distances, bad going that would knock weeks off vehicle endurance, no metalled roads over which to bring up supplies and a rail system that needed converting to European standard gauge. When the Panzers had crossed the Meuse in 1940 they at least had the Channel to aim for, but in Russia there was no such natural limit. One thing was clear: the campaign could only be won by destroying the Russian armies *where they stood*. They must not be allowed to escape into the depths of Russia and the only way to do this was with penetrations and encirclements made faster and deeper than ever before.

When tanks change hands – an enduring feature of armoured warfare. This British Matilda, taken over by the *Afrika Korps* after an earlier engagement, has just been recaptured by its rightful owners.

Into the postwar era with Russia's JS-3

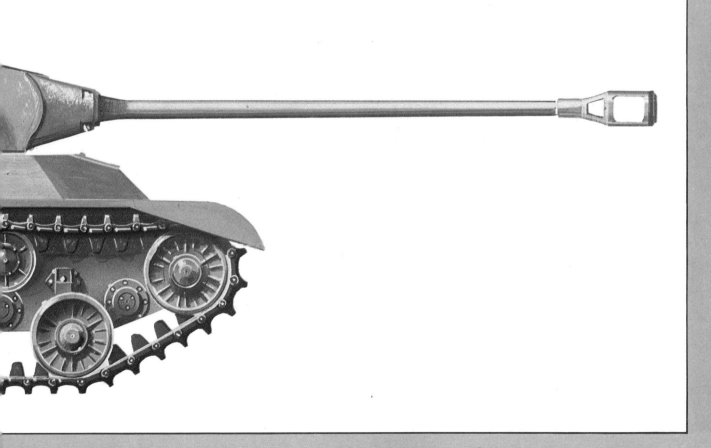

1941-1942: the Panzers invade Russia

FAR RIGHT Guderian in Russia directing the battle from his command vehicle, absorbed in the reports from the crews.

RIGHT Across the Desna, Russia 1941 (a PzKpfw III).

BELOW FAR RIGHT On into the endless void of Russia. PzKpfw IIIs cross the Don *en route* for Stalingrad, summer 1942.

BELOW A fine study of a PzKpfw IVF in Russia during the summer of 1942, showing the improved 75-mm gun, crew hatch on left side of turret, hull machine-gun mounting, and the spare track links pressed into service as supplementary armour on the outside of the hull.

The Germans were helped by the Red Army not having completed its tank refit. They gained total air supremacy on the first day and held it for months, they had combat experience, they had radio – they had the German *machine* of war, and although this sounds imprecise and melodramatic, a tremendous percentage of the Second World War poster propaganda was obsessed with the image of tanks and the men who fought in them. This professionalism won the classic Panzer victories at Bialystok, Minsk, Smolensk, Uman and Kiev – where such huge forces were trapped that it took weeks for the German infantry to finish the job – and cut the Red Army down to two-thirds of its prewar strength by the end of September. At Kiev alone, 500,000 men were killed or captured. By the time the battle for Moscow began in October, the Germans outnumbered the Russians for the first time, in men, guns and tanks.

What went wrong? German protagonists claim that Moscow must have fallen if the assault had been launched in August instead of October, instead of clearing the Ukraine first. The mud of the Russian autumn glued down the German advance; mobility was only restored by the frosts, when the weakened Panzer spearheads struggled to within distant sight of the Kremlin. But the Russians had the same weather to cope with. Their efforts to stand and hold on to western Russia won them just enough time to bring the Siberian armies west to join the front, to evacuate factories hundreds of miles to the east and push the production of tanks into overdrive. (During the first four months of 'Barbarossa', Russia's total industrial output had been halved.) Incredibly, by 5 December 1941 the Red Army defending Moscow outnumbered the Germans in everything but manpower. On that day Zhukov launched the first attack in the great Russian counter-offensive of 1941–2. After a year in which 2,391 Russian tanks had been destroyed, the Red Army's new tank divisions were attacking with a superiority of 531 machines (1,984 Russian to 1,453 German). German tank production for 1941 had hardly exceeded that of 1940, while Russian tank production – despite all the disasters and losses – turned out 2,996 of the new T-34 tank alone in 1941.

Germany could never win the tank production race with Russia, but Hitler's armies on the Eastern Front were still able to launch limited summer offensives in 1942 and 1943. In 1942 the twin objectives were the line of the Volga at Stalingrad and the oilfields of the Caucasus. Two Panzer armies were used, and used badly. One, the 1st, had to tackle the drive to the Caucasus without the assistance of the 4th Panzer Army. The latter could have rushed Stalingrad in late July, but was diverted to the south and then, belatedly, swung back to Stalingrad to help the 6th Army batter the place into submission. Stalingrad, like Verdun in the First World War, became a symbol of head-on combat with no quarter given or taken. In vain the Panzer commanders protested that tanks had never been designed for static fighting among the ruins. When the Russians bit off Stalingrad with a classic armoured 'pincer movement', they trapped not only the 6th Army but most of the 4th Panzer Army as well. When the end came in February 1943, the Germans had lost about 3500 armoured fighting vehicles in the Stalingrad ordeal since August 1942.

Given that German tank production could not match that of Soviet Russia, the German army in Russia should have assumed the defensive, hoarded its tanks in reserve, and refused to squander men or machines in 'last ditch' battles for unimportant places. Hitler, however, had other ideas.

Since the German invasion of Russia in June 1941, world tank development has never been the same. Every important tank feature – hitting-power, armoured protection, speed, agility and vulnerability of profile – has been largely decided by what Soviet Russia has produced. When the Panzers came up against the T-34 and the KV-1 in summer 1941 it was quite literally 'back to the drawing board' for the frantic production of the Panther (improving on many T-34 features) and the Tiger with the 88-mm gun. To which the Russians replied with the T-34/85 and the JS-2. To which the Germans replied with the King Tiger and so on. . . .

So we see again, and not for the last time, that the story of the tank is largely concerned with the eternal, escalating struggle between weapons and armour, which has also been the cause of a host of other developments in the weaponry of armoured warfare. It explained the use of the 88-mm AA gun against tanks, extempore at first but very soon routine, a legendary weapon (Allied tank men and infantry came to call just about everything explosive and fearful the work of '88s'). The 88-mm eventually became a tank gun with the German Tiger (PzKpfw VI) series. Self-propelled guns, pressed into service to give mobile artillery support to the infantry, were given high-velocity guns to make them specialized tank killers: tracked, armoured, turretless anti-tank guns.

Escalating tank armour resulted in a scramble for bigger and better orthodox anti-tank guns. The Germans dropped their original 37-mm PAK (*Panzer-abwehrkanone*) anti-tank gun in favour of the 50-mm and then the 75-mm gun; the British went from the 2-pounder to the 6-pounder and eventually the 17-pounder; they also used their versatile 25-pounder (88-mm) gun howitzer against tanks.

In turn, bigger and better anti-tank guns demanded better tank armour and tank silhouette design. Face-hardened plate, which broke up anti-tank shot on impact, was one such expedient; spaced armour was another. This gave the tank an outer armoured skin, a crinoline of 'skirt armour' to take the punch out of enemy shot before it could reach the main armour. Again, Russia's T-34 set new standards in sloped armour to deflect shot; tank silhouettes became lower and more streamlined as designers tried to improve shot deflection.

When the United States entered the war in December 1941, its native tank development was so out of touch with all these developments that even the worst tanks in service across the Atlantic would have given their American counterparts a rough time. American tank men were far luckier than the British in that they were not rushed into combat until better tanks had come along.

Twenty years of 'splendid isolation' had done terrible things to American inventiveness and originality as far as tanks were concerned. In 1940 American armoured fighting vehicle development was the most retarded in the world. Yet nothing speaks more highly in favour of the 'great arsenal of democracy' than the speed with which the cobwebs were swept away. By late summer 1941 the first crude American attempt at a modern tank was being welcomed by the British as infinitely preferable to their own designs – even though the British had had three years' combat experience and the Americans still had none at all. By the summer of 1942 the Americans had gone into mass-production with the M4 Sherman tank, mainstay of the British and American armoured forces until the end of the war and exported in thousands for years after 1945 – truly one of the top tank designs of all time.

By the end of 1940 the demands of the US army's cavalry lobby, plus the stubborn refusal to reconsider Christie's formula, meant that as far as tanks were concerned the American accent was on lightness and speed. The M2A1 had a scorching pace of 45 mph, albeit an armament of only three machine-guns. Its design was ludicrously different to contemporary European tank profiles; 'tall in the saddle', lofty and box-like, a lovely target for enemy guns if immobile for

PREVIOUS PAGES The staple tank of the western alliance: America's M4 Sherman, here seen in Normandy, 1944.

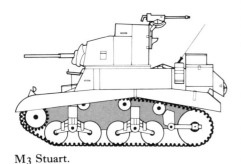

M3 Stuart.

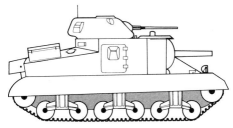

M3A Lee/Grant.

BELOW The awkward American Lee/Grant, the M3A, with its 75-mm gun fixed in the hull; but these tank men of the 8th Army seem only too happy to have, at last, a tank with enough hitting power to tackle Rommel's Panzers with confidence.

too long. The same applied to its successor, the M3A1 General Stuart, which had a 37-mm turret gun. The Stuart was accepted by the British as a Lend-Lease weapon and went into action a month before Pearl Harbor, in the western desert 'Crusader' offensive by the newly-formed 8th Army.

The Stuart's undoubted success was not won without a frightening price in knocked-out machines. Before 'Crusader' began on 18 November it was obvious that the Stuart had problems. It was undergunned by 1941 standards; it needed high-octane aviation fuel which put an extra burden on the fuel supply problem; it also had that dangerously lofty silhouette. Yet British tank crews were overjoyed to be given a tank whose tracks did *not* fall off or break, and which *was* mechanically reliable as well as supremely manoeuvrable. Battle-wise tank men used the Stuart's speed to compensate for the problem of having to run the gauntlet of 1800 yards of Panzer fire before it could get close enough for its 37-mm gun to knock out enemy tanks. A jinking, dodging approach at high speed made the Stuart a satisfyingly difficult target. Speed (double that of the Panzers) – reliability – excellent handling qualities – these made the Stuart blessed by the British tank crews, who christened it the 'Honey'.

American designers were never lured into planning super-heavy tanks for a very simple reason: American tanks would have to do their fighting overseas, and armoured colossi were not practicable as far as large-scale transportation was concerned. The attempts to design a modern medium tank were hampered by the fact that American technology was slow in producing a turret for mass-production that could carry a heavy gun. The M3A General Lee was obviously

Last variant of the accident-prone British Crusader – the Mk III with its 6-pounder gun, showing the co-axial Besa machine-gun.

influenced by the French Char-B: a 75-mm gun in the hull, a 37-mm gun in the turret. It went into production because there was nothing better at the time, and served with the British, like the Stuart, in the desert. Its silhouette was still too high, but at least it gave the British a tank with a decent-sized gun. 'Lord love you, what a job she is', exulted a British tank driver during the battle of Gazala in May 1942, surveying the dented but intact armour with satisfaction; 'And that gun there is a wizard. There's nothing wrong with the armour either.'

But the 'Grant', as it was known to the 8th Army, was never more than a stop-gap, a herald of far better things to come with the M4 Sherman, which was coming off the production lines by the disastrous high summer of 1942. Before the US army had been re-equipped with Shermans, 300 of them had to be packed off to Egypt to recoup the losses suffered by the 8th Army in the fighting since May. When a vastly strengthened and reinvigorated 8th Army attacked Rommel at Alamein in October 1942 it did so with a motley collection of Crusaders, Valentines, Stuarts, Grants and Shermans, with the Shermans the pick of the bunch. When the Alamein attack began there were 252 Shermans in the line and another 66 in reserve. The grand total of Montgomery's tank line-up at Alamein was 1,029 machines in the line: 252 Shermans, 170 Grants, 119 Stuarts, 194 Valentines and 294 Crusaders. Against this, Rommel had 31 Mk IIs, 85 Mk IIIs (short 50-mm guns), 88 Mk III Specials with high-velocity 50-mm guns, 8 Mk IVs (short 75-mm guns), and 30 Mk IV Specials with high-velocity 75-mm guns. Apart from seven command tanks he only had 23 Panzers, undergoing repair, in reserve. The Italian divisions fighting beside the *Afrika Korps* in Rommel's *Panzerarmee Afrika* contributed 298 light and medium tanks. Even with their doubtful assistance Rommel's tank men were facing odds of two to one when Alamein began, and the amazingly rapid development and production of the Sherman was largely responsible.

The Sherman itself was scheduled to be superseded in production by a heavier machine in 1943 but it proved to have so many excellent qualities that it was retained as the USA's main battle tank.

1942-1945: the Sherman, staple tank for the West

BELOW M4 Shermans stockpiled for the invasion of Europe.

ABOVE Shermans rolling onto the Normandy beaches from a tank-landing ship; and (right) providing new mounts for Chiang's re-equipped Chinese divisions in Burma.

Russia's superb T-34/76, with its
Christie-type suspension, thick sloped
armour and 76·2-mm gun.

Europe and the Mediterranean were the main tank battle areas in the Second
World War, but American machines also saw service in the Far East and
Pacific theatres. Stuarts were exported to China, where they provided adequate
opposition for Japan's *Chi-ha* Type 97. In the fight for the Pacific islands and
atolls, the Stuart was also useful in the primitive, infantry-support role, particularly in smashing Japanese blockhouses and pillboxes. On larger islands such as
Bougainville and Luzon, Saipan and Guam, both Shermans and Stuarts could
be effectively used. As for Burma, the low-priority status of that theatre was
signified by the fact that Lee tanks were still in service there in 1944–5, soldier-
ing nobly through the tremendous battles for Imphal, Kohima, Meiktila and
Mandalay, long after that tank had become totally obsolete in every other theatre
of the war. Burma was the last front to be re-equipped with Shermans.

The Americans proved much quicker than the British at experimenting with tracked and armoured self-propelled guns. Their 'Priest' gun with its formidable 105-mm gun showed up the British 'Bishop' – a Valentine hull with a 25-pounder mounted in a tall box on top – for the gimcrack confection that it was. A better blend of components was the 'Sexton', a Sherman hull with either a 75-mm gun or a 25-pounder. But the Americans learned much more from the Panzer divisions than the British in a much shorter time. One lesson as vital as it was obvious was the need for tank killers which could support orthodox tanks, and their M10 Tank Destroyer was unique. It used a Sherman hull as a platform for a 76-mm high velocity gun, but the latter (unlike the German *Panzerjäger* equivalents with their hull-mounted guns) was mounted in a fully traversing turret. There was a price to be paid – the turret was open to the sky and the side armour was flimsy – but for all that the versatile M10 and its successor, the M18 or 'Hellcat' were invaluable additions to American armoured strength.

American tanks in the Second World War had two other important advantages. The standard heavy machine-gun they carried, the ·50-inch, was superior to the lighter British ·303-inch, the German 7·9-mm and Russian 7·62-mm. The other advantage was a combination of America's enormous industrial and mass-production capacity (49,000 Shermans were built during the Second World War) and the USA's geographical/strategic position, which meant that her tanks had to be of reasonable dimensions, suitable for shipping overseas in bulk. This effectively prevented American tank designers from wasting time on excessively bulky super-heavies. And it is worth remembering that the only tanks shipped to Russia from the west which were welcome gifts were Grants and Shermans – and even they fell short of the Russian ideal.

Low cost, highest possible production, maximum speed, fire-power and armour, no irrelevant fussing about the comfort and endurance of the crews – such was the Russian approach. The way it worked out can be judged by comparing the vital statistics of the first two marks of the T-34 and the Sherman – bearing in mind that the T-34 entered service a year before the Sherman.

	T-34/76A	Sherman M4A1
Weight	26·3 tons	30·2 tons
Crew	4	5
Armament	76·2-mm + 2 mg	75-mm + 3 mg
Armour	65 mm max., 15 mm min.	75 mm max., 15 mm min.
Max. Speed	32 mph	25 mph
Dimensions: Length	21' 7"	19' 8½"
Width	9' 10"	8' 9"
Height	8'	9' 9"

Thus the T-34 was lighter, longer, lower, faster, and harder-hitting than the Sherman. What the figures do not show is that the T-34's armoured protection was vastly superior because of its near-perfect sloping, nor that Russian mass-production made T-34 an ideal medium for cannibalization. T-34 turrets were used as pillboxes and were also fitted to gunboats and armoured trains. T-34's speed was another vital asset – the author still cherishes the salty comments of an ex-Luftwaffe 88-mm gunner trying to explain the stark terror of being at the business end of the best anti-tank gun in service, while at the same time being virtually unable to draw a bead on T-34s advancing flat-out across country.

Yet the above comparisons only scratch the surface. The very best tank designs allow for the maximum improvements to be made to an initial model without having to scrap the production line and start work on a completely new tank. This is how T-34 and Sherman designs measured up in 1944, and the figures tell a startling story:

	T-34/85	Sherman M3A4 3E8
Weight	32 tons	32 tons
Crew	5	5
Armament	85-mm + 2 mg	76-mm + 3 mg
Armour	90 mm max., 20 mm min.	64 mm max., 19 mm min.
Max. Speed	32 mph	32 mph
Dimensions: Length	24′ 9″	24′ 8″
Width	9′ 10″	8′ 9″
Height	7′ 11″	11′ 2$\frac{7}{8}$″

Parity had only been reached in tank weight, the number of crew and optimum speed. But look at the hitting-power – an 85 mm gun as against a 76 mm gun – and protection, the Russian tank with 90 mm and the American with 64 mm, the crew of T-34 enjoying the frontal security of a full inch more front armour plate than their allies. As for profile vulnerability – how much of its height a tank shows when concealed in static deployment – T-34 had lost an inch while Sherman had gained nearly 2 feet 5 inches of height. (See Appendix II.)

The same features applied to the Soviet heavies: the KV-I, the JS-2 (Josef Stalin 2) and the JS-3. The American contemporary of JS-3, appearing in the last six months of the war in Europe, was the Pershing, delayed by two years because of the decision to concentrate on the mass-production of the Sherman. Pershing's main armament was the 90-mm gun and its maximum armour thickness was 110 mm; JS-3 had the 122-mm gun and a maximum armour thickness of 200 mm.

When T-34 and KV-I had made their debuts during the disastrous summer of 1941, when it seemed that the entire Red Army must be swept from the board by Christmas, it was not easy to see that Russian tank designers had in fact won a major victory. This victory may be compared to Britain's launch of the *Dreadnought* in 1906: a revolutionary new design which made all the best German equivalents obsolete. The Germans came back with designs of their own which were individually superior but rendered strategically hopeless by being grossly outnumbered.

As far as *matériel* was concerned, the Russians retained the initiative. Their tanks were so formidable that the Germans experimented wildly with a bewildering choice of ersatz tracked tank-killers and assault guns. They mounted 75-mm guns in PzKpfw III chassis (*Sturmgeschütz* III) and in Czech 38ts ('Hetzer'). The 88-mm was mounted on the PzKpfw IV ('Nashorn') and the Tiger ('Elefant'). Captured Russian 76·2-mm guns, rechambered, were married to the Czech 38t chassis to produce 'Marder'. Even the chassis of the little

LEFT Successor to the KV was the JS-2 with its prodigious 122-mm gun.

BELOW Rommel faces up to the enormous problem of defending the Atlantic coast of France (spring 1944). In the background is a typical German self-propelled gun: a 'Lorraine' composite, with a 105-mm howitzer on a captured French Hotchkiss tank hull.

PzKpfw II was used to carry a 105-mm howitzer ('Wespe'). The Germans ended the war by producing tank-killing variants of their own best tanks: *Jagdpanther*, with an 88-mm on a Panther chassis, and *Jagdtiger*, a 128-mm gun on a Tiger chassis.

All this ingenuity distracted from the main German tank programme. The machines produced were, moreover, *defensive* in concept. The Russians never bothered. They kept their self-propelled artillery down to four basic types: SU-76 (76 mm), SU-100 (100 mm), JSU-122 (122 mm) and JSU-152 (152 mm), making for maximum simplicity of production as well as more than adequate hitting-power. They preferred to turn out a flood of *offensive* armoured fighting vehicles rather than waste time on *defensive* tank-killers whose *raison d'être* was to stalk, ambush, harass and delay the enemy's armoured assault.

And yet in the last analysis the outcome in the east was not decided by the quality of the weapons alone. As the initiative in the Second World War passed to the Allies it became clearer than ever that the thickness of a tank's armour, the calibre of its guns, were useless without human material of equally specialized quality.

7 The Defeat of the Panzers

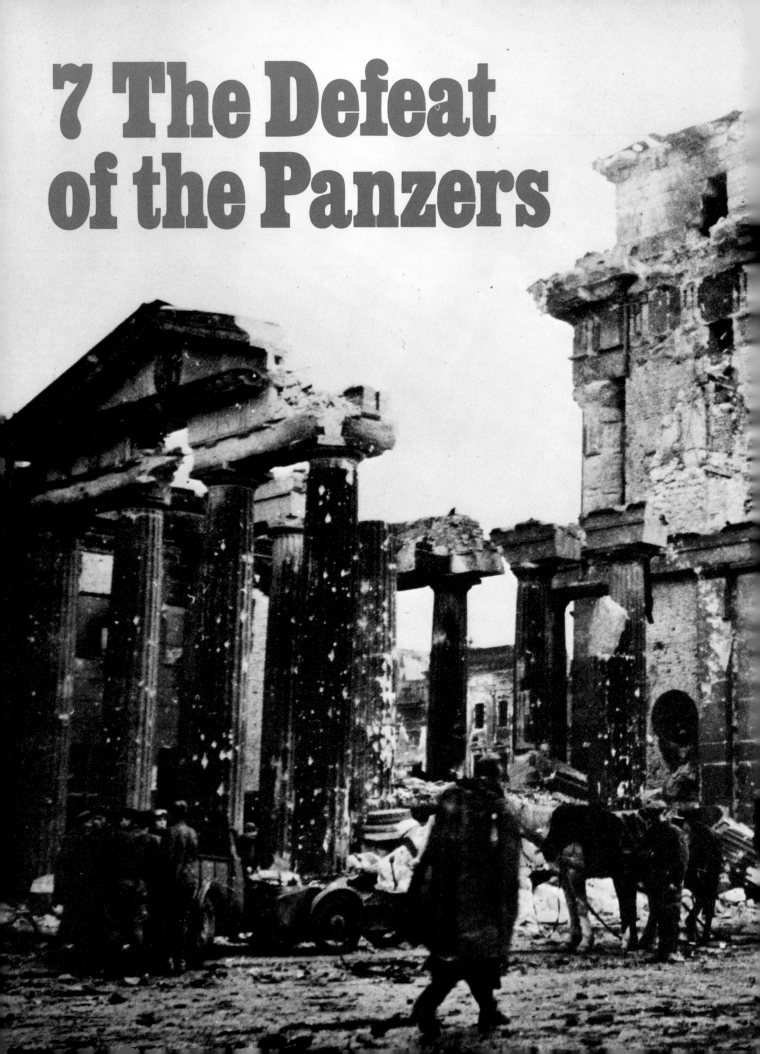

Fortunately for the Allies, German tank production did not reach top gear until the high summer of 1944, when it was too late. The British and Americans landed in Normandy, the Red Army destroyed the German Army Group Centre in Russia, and the vice began to close. But the last generation of the Third Reich's Panzers were emphatic proof of how quickly tank escalation in warfare can produce superb machines as well as ill-conceived and ineffective white elephants.

After 1942, the disastrous year of Stalingrad, even Hitler accepted the need for a total overhaul of German tank production and allocation. Guderian, sacked at the height of the battle of Moscow for insisting that retreat was essential, was brought back as Inspector-General of Armoured Troops. Guderian wanted 1943 to be a year of strict defensive in the east. He wanted no more Panzer divisions formed until all existing ones had been brought up to full combat efficiency (a condition they had not enjoyed since 1940) with the new Panthers and Tigers, that had been rigorously tested and purged of teething troubles. He wanted the tracked assault guns, jealously monopolized by the artillery arm, to be transferred to the Panzer arm in order to give the Panzer divisions their own mobile, armoured artillery. Above all he wanted to build up a reserve pool of tanks big enough to handle war on two fronts when the inevitable came and the western allies launched their invasion. Again fortunately for the Allies, he got none of these things.

After the front had been ripped open at Stalingrad, the ensuing Russian flood had been abruptly shut off by a brilliant Panzer campaign masterminded by Field-Marshal Erich von Manstein. Using comparatively small forces, but always in local superiority and when and where least expected, Manstein forced the Russians to abandon their westward lunge. By hooking repeatedly at the Russian flanks, he stitched up the Eastern Front from south to north. The *rasputitsa* (Russia's spring and autumn answer to the monsoon, when the Russian terrain dissolves in mud) of spring 1943 halted mobile operations before the westward-bulging salient around Kursk could be reduced. This salient came to obsess Hitler, who ordered it to be the target for the German 1943 summer offensive – with Guderian and the other Panzer experts going down on their knees in efforts to get the Führer to see sense.

For the Kursk attack the Germans had the Mk III and Mk IV Specials, with skirts of outer armour and high-velocity 50-mm and 75-mm guns. They had the first Panthers (75-mm gun) and Tigers (88-mm gun), and the Elefant or 'Ferdinand'. This misbegotten monster was little more than a refined testbed for the Porsche variant of the Tiger tank: a lumbering self-propelled gun armed with the 88-mm. It was utterly useless because it had no machine-guns with which to neutralize enemy infantry and gunners in close-quarter combat. 'They literally had to go quail-shooting with cannons,' fumed Guderian, who loathed the things but had to use them because, thanks to Hitler's enthusiasm, they were there.

The Panther was another matter. It was Germany's answer to the T-34 and looked it, with a long, protruding 75-mm gun, sloped armour (110 mm maximum), excellent performance across rough terrain and a speed of 34 mph. But few of these excellent attributes had been perfected by the summer of 1943. The Panthers were subject to breakdowns and their fuel system was inadequate, transforming a tank from a fighting machine to a funeral pyre for the crew when hit. The big Tigers had different problems: they were too big and too slow and could be easily killed from the flank.

For the Panzer experts, however, the most horrifying thing about the Kursk attack was the complete abandonment of the fundamental principle of armoured strategy. Massed tanks were a winner when flung at the enemy's point of maximum *weakness,* not strength. Sending them against defences which were waiting for the attack was suicide – Stalingrad had proved that. When 'Citadel',

PREVIOUS PAGES A Red Army JS-2 by the Brandenburg Gate in ruined Berlin, May 1945.

Tiger I.

ABOVE Germany's answer to the T-34: the excellent Panther (PzKpfw V), one of the best tanks of the war, with sloped armour and a long, high-velocity 75-mm gun. But by the time the Panther appeared in 1943 the Russians had up-gunned the T-34 to 85-mm.

LEFT Guderian, entrusted with the overhaul of the Panzer arm after the Stalingrad disaster, casts a critical eye over an early specimen of the new PzKpfw VI heavy: the Tiger, with its 88-mm gun.

A T-34 advances with Russian infantry in the Orel-Kursk battle of July 1943, which ruined all Guderian's hopes of amassing a powerful armoured reserve.

the Kursk attack, finally went in on 4 July 1943 the Russians had been expecting it for months and had prepared three deep belts of anti-tank defences modelled on the best German lines. Both north and south of the salient, the Germans were halted and the Panzers subjected to near static warfare, the negation of their true role. When the assault was called off on 13 July 'the greatest tank battle in history', in which more than 5400 armoured fighting vehicles had been involved, was over. But the defeat of the Panzers had not been inflicted in a tank versus tank duel – as far as tank armament was concerned the Germans had the advantage. The 1800 Panzers which attacked at Kursk were repelled not only by 3600 Russian tanks, but by 6000 anti-tank guns and 400,000 mines.

At Kursk, a new menace for the tank emerged for the first time on the Eastern Front: the tank-busting aircraft. The Germans gave a new lease of life to the ungainly Stuka dive-bomber by hanging 37-mm cannon under its wings and using it against tanks, together with the Henschel Hs-129. One of the *Luftwaffe*'s most unorthodox aces was Hans-Ulrich Rudel, whose speciality was tank-busting: he knocked out 12 Russian tanks on the first day of 'Citadel' alone, and by the end of the war had raised his score to 510 tanks destroyed. The British could claim to have been first in this field, using tank-busting Hurricane IIs with 20-mm cannon in North Africa. This new menace from the sky pointed a new moral for men who fought in tanks: control of the air over the battlefield was now a vital ingredient of survival, never mind victory.

Kursk had been preceded in miniature by events in North Africa, where the retreating *Afrika Korps* had fought its last battles. After the British and Americans landed in Rommel's rear, Rommel had turned on the green American forces in Tunisia and introduced them to Panzer warfare by attacking at Kasserine Pass (14–15 February 1943). He pushed a frightening dent into the Allied front, but disagreements and misunderstandings with his colleague von Arnim let the opportunity slip and the British managed to hold him. When Rommel, tired, sick and on the verge of recall, turned on Montgomery at Medenine (6 March), he launched a lacklustre Panzer attack straight down the throat of Montgomery's anti-tank defences and lost 50 irreplaceable tanks for absolutely no gain.

The last phase of the campaign, the fight for the bridgehead around Tunis and Bizerta, ended on 13 May 1943 with the surrender of nearly 250,000 Axis troops. It was largely an infantry battle with tanks used in support, and sending the newest battalion of Tiger tanks into the cauldron was little more than a propaganda exercise. Certainly its drawbacks were immediately apparent to the British and Americans: there was little future, amid the hills and valleys of

Tigers moving up to the front, East Prussia. March 1945.

FAR RIGHT Parade of British Valentines in captured Tripoli, 1943: a final bow in active service. The Valentine's problem was that its turret design prevented it from being updated by being given a gun heavier than the 40-mm 2-pounder.

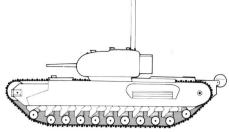

Churchill.

BELOW The brutal cost of finding out how *not* to land tanks on defended beaches: the Churchill's disastrous debut at Dieppe in 1942.

Tunisia, for a tank too heavy for most bridges, too wide for tracks under $12\frac{1}{4}$ feet across, and too slow to take advantage of the convolutions of the terrain by dashing in and out of cover. The British knocked out their first Tiger on 31 January 1943, with 6-pounder anti-tank guns, and as the British Official History frostily comments, 'an immediate and accurate technical examination led to a sound appreciation of the tank's powers and limitations.'

Certainly the British needed all the help they could get in tank design, for by 1943 their own approach was wandering down an erratic and depressing path of inadequacy. The infantry Mk IV, the Churchill, had been mooted in 1940, that halfway date in tank design when the Char-B and the American Lee/Grant design still retained a heavy gun in the hull and a light turret gun. Delays in actual production had removed the hull by the time the Churchill saw its first action in August 1942 in the raid on Dieppe. In no way was this a fair test, but despite the murderous losses among the Canadian troops it taught some invaluable lessons in landing tanks that were not forgotten. Putting infantry ashore without simultaneous tank assistance was obviously suicidal. The beach surface would have to be thought of – deep shingle could halt a tank as efficiently as mud. The men in the assault wave also needed a weapon to cope with obstacles and pillboxes. And the end product was a host of special-duty tanks with widely-differing tasks – the so-called 'Funnies', which spearheaded the liberation of Europe.

The Churchill replaced the Valentine in 1942–3, relegating the latter to training. The Valentine's problems had always centred on its modest size, effectively precluding its up-gunning from the little 2-pounder turret gun. Churchill was an ugly, obsolete-looking design, all square angles and vertical surfaces offering 'traps' for enemy shot – but at least it was big enough to allow a wide range of modifications to the basic design. It was also very well armoured, though with those boxy lines it had to be and the speed suffered in consequence:

1944: the 'Funnies', custom-built to crack the Atlantic Wall

BELOW Churchill AVRE. This particular machine, exhumed in Normandy in late 1976, is scheduled to remain there as a D-Day memorial.

RIGHT The DD swimming tank (this is a Valentine trainer) with its flotation screen raised, enabling fighting tanks to hit the beaches with the first-wave of assault troops.

FAR RIGHT Sherman Crab flail tank used to cut lanes through minefields.

ABOVE Churchill Crocodile, the flamethrower tank, which carried its napalm in an armoured trailer for safety.

RIGHT Churchill Bobbin, laying a firm carpet to enable follow-up tanks and vehicles to cross soft sand dunes.

	Valentine I	Churchill VII
Weight	16 tons	40 tons
Crew	3	5
Armament	2-pounder + 2 mg	75-mm + 3 mg
Armour	65 mm max., 30 mm min.	152 mm max., 19 mm min.
Speed	15 mph	$13\frac{1}{2}$ mph
Dimensions: Length	17′ 9″	24′ 2″
Width	7′ 6″	10′ $10\frac{1}{2}$″
Height	7′ $5\frac{1}{2}$″	8′ $10\frac{1}{4}$″

With the Valentine at hand for trying out ideas in prototype, the Sherman and Churchill were the two main models for the development of specialized armour for D-Day in Normandy. The Sherman 'Duplex Drive' or DD was a swimming tank, with twin screws powered by its engine, suspended in the water by a collapsible canvas screen. When it touched the beach the drive was switched from the screws to the tracks and the screen was dropped, allowing the turret gun to come instantly into action. The DD meant that the first men to hit the beach would have tanks along with them, which could take on the German beach defences from the water's edge.

With Rommel in charge of the German coastal defences it was obvious that dense minefields would have to be dealt with, as at Alamein, before men and machines could push inland. The 'Crab' minesweeping tank was a refinement of the earlier 'Baron' and 'Scorpion' devices that had been tried out in North Africa: a Sherman fitted with twin booms carrying a drum with chain flails. With the drum powered by the tank's engine, the Crab could advance behind its flailing chains, touching off mines in its path and clearing a gap through the minefield.

To cope with pillboxes and blockhouses there was the Churchill AVRE ('Armoured Vehicle, Royal Engineers'), which carried a 25-pound spigot mortar. This 'Flying Dustbin' was a stand-off demolition charge which packed a devastating punch against fixed defences. (In November 1976, as this book was nearing completion, an AVRE was discovered at Courseulles in Normandy; it is to be restored and displayed as a D-Day monument.)

'Bobbin' was another Churchill variant to enable follow-up tanks and vehicles to get past stretches of soft going. It carried a drum of matting 'carpet' 10 feet long, over which the tank could crawl as the carpet was unrolled. Then there was the 'Canal Defence Light' or CDL with a brilliant searchlight to dazzle and illuminate the enemy at night, which promised better than it performed; the 'Crocodile', a flame-throwing Churchill tank; the 'Ark', a Churchill which could drop a box girder bridge over an anti-tank ditch; and the 'Bullshorn plough', intended to throw up mines on either side of a tank advancing into a minefield.

Such were the Funnies, the specialized tanks in the Allied armoury for D-Day. Their unfailing patron was Britain's 'Guderian', the explosive, brilliant Major-General Sir Percy Hobart, blocked and pilloried by the establishment of the British Army High Command who feared and distrusted him, but second to

Massed T-34/85s roar in to the assault with waves of infantry in the great Russian summer offensive of 1944.

none as a trainer of armoured divisions and sponsor of any idea that would make tanks more effective.

During the battle for Normandy a new variant appeared, the hedgecutting tank, which consisted of two stout, sharp prongs on the front of a Sherman. This was born of the obstacle posed by the Normandy *bocage*: a high earth bank topped with a hedge, perfect for defending infantry and anti-tank gunners. With the hedge-cutter a tank could drive straight into the bank and hedge, punching clean through with its own momentum and emerging into open country on the other side to the discomfiture of the Germans.

Total, merciless Allied air supremacy prevented the Germans from moving by day during the fight for Normandy. ('If it's black it's British, if it's silver it's American, if you don't see it at all it's the *Luftwaffe*', was the bitter watchword of the German troops in Normandy.) In the weeks before and after the invasion long-range Allied bombers pounded the roads and railways behind the invasion zone, making it impossible for the Germans to move in reinforcements to throw the Allies back into the sea.

In their incredible mass breakthroughs and enormous territorial advances of 1943–5, the Red Army used no such expedients. After the war, Eisenhower asked Zhukov, the top Russian commander of the Second World War, how it had been done. Ike was appalled at Zhukov's reply. The British and Americans always used to give the game away by preliminary mine-clearing operations, said Zhukov; the Red Army attacked as though the mines did not exist. The first wave of infantry would suffer terrible losses; the second wave would also be badly hurt, though less so than the first – but the third wave would invariably break clean through with the tanks on their heels. Another Russian tactic was to lay down a furious bombardment on strips of the German front line, leaving lanes along which Russian infantry and tanks would advance while their own shells were still falling. Before the Germans realized it, the attacking Russians could be a couple of miles into the German rear areas – but this could mean the attackers having to accept 75 per cent losses from their own shells for a while. Tactics like this enabled the Red Army to 'tear the guts out of the German army', in Churchill's phrase, but any western general who had tried it would have been dismissed, court-martialled, execrated and generally broken for life. Even the final battle for Berlin (16 April–8 May 1945), according to Soviet sources, cost the Red Army 'about 300,000 men killed, wounded or missing, over 2000 tanks or self-propelled guns, and more than 500 aircraft'. Such losses are directly comparable to those suffered in the trapped Soviet pocket at Smolensk in the terrible summer of 1941 – and this was with total air supremacy and a crushing supremacy in tanks.

By contrast, the struggle for Normandy – including the losses on D-Day itself – cost the British and Americans overall casualties of 209,672 (36,976 of them killed) between 6 June and 25 August – an amazingly small price to pay for gaining a foothold in Europe, re-opening a western front against Germany, and effectively destroying the German field armies between the Atlantic coast and the frontier of the Reich.

This is not to say that the Normandy battle was a walk-over for the Allies: German resistance was much faster and tougher than had been bargained for and the whole schedule of the invasion was thrown out of gear. (The city of Caen was supposed to be taken on D-Day; in fact its ruins were not securely in Allied hands until D + 36.) To break the deadlock Montgomery used the Caen sector as a magnet to attract the bulk of the German armour, where the crack *Waffen*-SS Panzer crews in their Tigers and Panthers had a field day at the expense of the out-gunned and repeatedly ambushed Shermans and Churchills of the British armoured divisions. One ace Tiger crew, that of *Hauptsturmführer* Michel Wittman, knocked out 25 British tanks in one morning. But this one-sided slugging-match, deliberately undertaken on ground unfavourable to Allied armour, thinned out the opposition on the western sector of the Normandy bridgehead and allowed Patton's tanks to break out successfully on 25 July.

Patton was the master of breakneck pursuit, driving his men and machines without mercy – a constant headache, as Rommel had been in North Africa, to his high command. 'My boys can eat their belts,' he urged, 'but my tanks gotta have gas.' The advances made by his 3rd Army rivalled and excelled those made by Guderian in 1940 and 1941. All Patton's best qualities closely resembled those of Rommel and Guderian: relentless drive, the urge to press an advantage to the full, and calculated insubordination to cautious orders from on top.

General 'Blood 'n' Guts' Patton, America's master of the armoured advance: 'My boys can eat their belts, but my tanks gotta have gas.'

In the great battles of 1944, Allied tanks on both Eastern and Western Fronts faced a new danger. This was the rocket missile, firing a bomb with a hollow-charge warhead. The hollow-charge missile was a revolutionary step in the contest of weapons versus armour. It did not need a high-velocity gun to speed it to the target. The cone-shaped hollow with its metal liner, when detonated, turned inside-out and focused a stream of gas and liquid metal on the armour, melting straight through with terrible effects on the crew inside. The Germans were first in the field with their *Panzerschreck* and *Panzerfaust* missile launchers, followed closely by the Americans with the bazooka. Britain's contribution was the PIAT ('Projectile Infantry Anti-Tank'). With all variants there were snags. The bomb had to hit squarely to be sure of a kill; the range of the rocket was short (under 100 yards), and as tanks were nearly always accompanied by watchful infantry this made the 'stalk' highly dangerous. In ideal conditions, however, the hollow-charge projector was very effective and one of the most novel antidotes was developed by the Russians. Their tank crews would search houses, rip out bed-frames and mount the mesh of bedsprings on the front of their tanks – a crude but effective 'torpedo net' that stopped the hollow charge from bursting directly on the tank's armour. Lengths of timber on turret and hull, which could be blown away without damaging the tank, were another Russian anti-*Panzerfaust* expedient.

If tank hunting with the new rocket missiles was dangerous, the use of magnetic anti-tank limpet mines was positively suicidal against tanks in company or supported by infantry. Yet it remained a threat until the end of the war, and both the Germans and the Russians took to plastering their tanks with anti-magnetic paste to prevent enemy heroes placing limpet mines. (A well-placed charge of explosive, jammed under a turret overhang, could blow the whole turret off.)

The partnership of Guderian and Albert Speer, Reich Minister of Arms and Munitions from August 1942, had done amazing things for Panzer production. In June 1940 the monthly output of all types had been 121. In June 1941 it was 310 and had only crept marginally up to 378 by the time of the battle of Moscow in December. A year later, when the 6th Army and the 4th Panzer Army were fighting for their lives at Stalingrad, it had risen to 760. But in 1943 and 1944, despite the massive Allied bombing, Panzer production rocketed to 1,229 in December 1943 and an all-time record of 1,669 in July 1944. (The figures are from *US Strategic Bombing Survey*, 'Economic Report'.) The trouble was that the bombings did successfully disrupt the road and rail transport net of the Third Reich and the occupied territories, and broke the back of Germany's fuel production and supply, which meant that the new tanks could not be rushed to where they were most needed and were always starved of fuel when they did get there.

For all that, the Germans continued to produce excellent tanks and their last winner was the Tiger II or King Tiger with its well-sloped armour. Again mounting the 88-mm gun, King Tiger's frontal armour was a massive 185 mm. It could make 15·7 mph on roads and 12 mph cross-country in good going, but its main problem was its weight of 68·65 tons, a major problem in soft going and

Far too late to avert defeat, German production of armour reaches its peak in the summer of 1944.

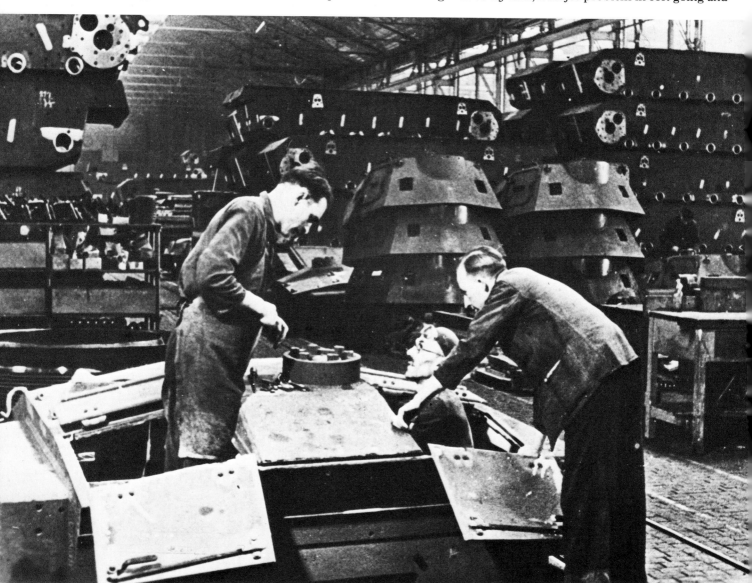

when crossing bridges. Extended battle tracks gave King Tiger a better 'footing' but increased its width to 12 feet 3⅝ inches. It never got the chance to show what it could do in open country and good going; its debut *en masse* was the German counter-offensive in the Ardennes of December 1944, the 'battle of the Bulge', when it had to operate along narrow, snow-and-slush-choked roads and inadequate bridges.

The only tank the Allies had which could tackle King Tiger was the 'Firefly' hybrid, the Sherman carrying the British 17-pounder gun. In the last months of the war in Europe the new American heavy, delayed by concentration on Sherman production, finally reached the front. This was the M-26 Pershing with its 90-mm gun and maximum armour of 101·6 mm. Only 20 Pershings saw action before the end of the war in Europe.

To accompany the Panther and Tiger tanks the Germans concentrated on three self-propelled tank hunters in the last eighteen months of the war. *Jagdpanzer* Hetzer carried a 75-mm gun on the old Czech 38t chassis; production began in December 1943 and 1,577 were completed. *Jagdpanther* was the 88-mm gun on a Panther tank chassis, 382 of which were completed; and *Jagdtiger* was the 128-mm gun on a Tiger chassis.

Sherman Firefly.

Wooden mockup of the lunatic fringe *Maus* project: a 188-ton colossus.

Jagdtiger, however, reflected the old, fatal distraction which had always bedevilled armoured fighting vehicle design: the obsession with weight and hitting-power at the expense of manoeuvrability. To build a tank hunter which was even slower and just as bulky as your own best tank made no kind of sense. Nor did the waste of time and effort on two other illogical behemoths: the *Sturmmörser* Tiger, or *Sturmtiger*, which fired a 15-inch rocket mortar shell but needed a crane to load it; and the ludicrous *Maus*. This was to have a weight of 188 tons, a maximum speed of 12 mph, 240 mm of armour, and no less than *two* turret guns, a 128-mm and a co-axial 75-mm. *Maus* never got past the wooden mockup stage, and even if it had it could never have been mass-produced – nor could it have been of the slightest use on the battlefield. Hitler of course, loved the idea; he had once horrified Guderian by asking whether or not the 32-inch railway gun could be used against tanks. 'It could be fired at them, I dare say, but it could certainly never hit one,' was Guderian's reply.

But Hitler and the German super-heavy fanatics were by no means alone. The British produced what can only be described as an armoured 'thing': Tortoise, weighed down by 225 mm of armour, 78 tons in weight, carrying a 94-mm AA gun but only capable of 12 mph. Nor was Tortoise a true tank:

designed as a super-heavy tank destroyer, its gun was mounted in the hull, not in a turret. Conceived in 1942, it took four years to complete, missed the Second World War completely and was mercifully abandoned. The American T-28 was a similar experiment with a 105-mm gun, but no less pointless.

The British equivalent of the *Maus*, the equally absurd but aptly-named Tortoise.

What were the basic reasons for the eclipse of the Panzers after their runaway string of victories in 1939–41?

First came quality, the refusal by Hitler to accept that a few armoured divisions at full combat strength were always a better proposition than a lot of watered-down ones. It was not until 1943 that Guderian was able to start trying to restore full combat efficiency to the Panzer divisions and even then he never fully succeeded. Nor were the rigid inter-service demarcations of the *Wehrmacht* any help. The *Luftwaffe* was responsible for anti-aircraft guns (which included the all-important '88'); the artillery claimed that self-propelled guns were its prerogative. Thus, although the weapons were there, they were never used at maximum efficiency.

Second came industrial capacity and output. It is still hard to accept that Nazi Germany only moved on to a full war footing in late 1942. The Allies produced more tanks and got them to the front quicker, which meant that superior German tanks and tank tactics were always chasing the infinite. The classic example (p. 86) was the immediate delivery of 300 Shermans to the western desert after the destruction of the 8th Army's tank force at Gazala and Tobruk in May–June 1942. Six months before, Rommel's Panzers had wrought havoc with the inferior British and American tanks during the 'Crusader' fighting, but the Allied reinforcements kept coming and it was Rommel who had to call off the battle and retreat.

Third was the problem of production and conversion to new machines. Once committed to the PzKpfw III and IV, German tank production could not be converted overnight to turning out Panthers and Tigers to combat the T-34s and KVs. This was a problem which the British and Americans also had; the Russians had an easier task because of their insistence on simplicity, concentration on one proven type; and the draconian conditions of Soviet labour (which would never have been tolerated for a minute by the trade unions of

Britain and America) enabled them to achieve miracles of production beyond the wildest dreams of any other combatant power.

During the great run of classic Panzer victories, all of the following conditions had been present:

1. German armour operated as self-contained divisions, not doled out to give infantry units support or split up into brigades or smaller mobile columns.

2 German air supremacy had been paramount, dominating the skies over the battlefield, bombing far behind the Allied front, shooting up Allied relief columns and troops on the move, and acting in close tactical co-operation with the Panzer forces.

3 Threatening Allied countermoves had been best handled by luring the Allied tanks into chosen ground and destroying them with well-sited anti-tank guns.

4 The weather and terrain had been such as to get the maximum performance out of armoured formations on the move.

In every case where the Panzer divisions were committed to street fighting amid shattered buildings, or forced to operate without adequate air cover, on unsuitable terrain or in impossible weather conditions for tank movements, victory eluded them.

As far as the tanks themselves were concerned the following basic principles applied, and still do:

1. A tank is an offensive weapon, designed for mobile warfare. It is not designed to be used as a static pillbox.

2. This being the case it is expected to face the most damaging fire head-on, and so its toughest armour is on the front of the hull and turret.

3. It must have sufficient armour and hitting-power to stand up to its opposite numbers in a tank-versus-tank encounter.

4. Its surface should offer as few right-angled planes as possible to enemy shot, and the tank should also show as little of itself as possible when in a concealed firing position.

5. It should have maximum speed to get out of trouble when necessary, plus manoeuvrability to prevent itself from being attacked in flank or rear.

6. It should have sufficient machine-guns to cope with enemy infantry and keep the latter at bay, and preferably a co-axial machine-gun in the turret which, firing tracer bullets, helps pinpoint the target for the gunner.

7. It may well be in action for weeks at a time without respite, which means that excessively cramped conditions will cause premature crew fatigue. This also underlines the need for a high standard of mechanical reliability.

8. The crew must know that if their tank is hit and set on fire they will be able to bale out instantly without being roasted to death.

9. Not every knocked-out tank is a write-off. Tank recovery units must operate as far forward as possible, retrieving damaged and abandoned tanks and either repairing them at field workshops or sending them back to the rear.

10. No tank has ever been designed without a crop of teething troubles, and no new model should be rushed into premature action before these problems have been solved. By ignoring this principle, both Churchill and Hitler were guilty of condemning hundreds of tank crews to unnecessary deaths.

When it came to meeting all these requirements the Germans were the most individually successful of all the combatant powers, followed by the Russians, to whom the human requirements of tank warfare were always secondary. As far as the British and Americans were concerned, their weaknesses complemented each other. British battle tanks never achieved the excellence of Panther or Tiger, but they were more than adequate as base material for the offbeat

Funnies, the specialized armour. The faults of the American Sherman were cancelled out by the numbers produced, and the success of the Sherman Firefly symbolized the effectiveness of Anglo-British collaboration. Together the British and Americans evolved an efficient pattern of backup services to keep the tanks moving, though the Allies found – as Kleist's Panzers had experienced during the dash to the Caucasus in 1942 – that runaway advances could outstrip fuel and ammunition supplies, come to a halt from sheer exhaustion, and give the enemy enough time to recover.

From late 1942 the western Allies never lost air supremacy until the end of the war and in general used it well, but there were exceptions. Tactical bombing could be disastrously erratic, falling on friend and foe alike; and it was often used indiscriminately and stupidly, as at Monte Cassino, when the destruction of the monastery only created an impassable lunar landscape of rubble and made the job of the German defenders far easier than it had been.

Above all, however, the tank warfare of the Second World War proved that the heady prophesies of the tank pioneers had been justified. Tanks did make the bloodbaths of 1914–8 a thing of the past; tanks were, as Guderian put it, 'a life-saving weapon'; and tanks could be the prime instrument of victory in battle. But they could not do it on their own. Operating as a team, they were themselves part of a larger team. A tank can win ground for its own side to occupy, but it only commands a very small area of its surroundings – and a tank without fuel or ammunition is a sophisticated junk-heap. In terms of strategy, 'tank battles' which put the enemy on the run but which are not exploited correctly are as pointless as any other wasted victory. The correct use of tanks is that of concentrated strength against a point of weakness, but this is only a means to an end and not an end in itself. If the strength is not enough, if it is directed half-heartedly or unwisely, disaster will follow as the night follows day; and the defeat of the Panzers between 1942 and 1945 proved this conclusively.

FOLLOWING PAGES The mailed fist of the world's top armoured force: Russian T-54s in Prague, August 1968.

8 Allied Victory, Cold War

No victory has ever created more problems for peacemakers than that of 1945. Of the completeness of Germany's defeat there was no doubt: the country was prostrate, and the Allies had no difficulty in carving up Germany into occupation zones and policing them. But too many comfortable assumptions had been made about Stalin's postwar attitude to reconstruction and self-determination in the liberated states of Europe. Russia had not only survived the German onslaught to become the main instrument of victory over Germany's land forces: she now held the whole of eastern Europe and refused to let go. By contrast, all the western Allies wanted to do was to see to it that Germany was safely trussed, then go home *en masse* and demobilize.

No country in the world needed demobilization and reconstruction as badly as Russia – and no country in the world proved able to demobilize 1,800,000 soldiers (the incredible equivalent of 325 divisions), reduce her annual production of tanks and other armoured fighting vehicles from 30,000 to 5000 a year, and still keep a million armed men outside her borders. It was a terrifying situation, kept stable only by the fact that America had the atom bomb. Not even the rapid establishment of nuclear parity and stalemate could change the fact that the West could not, on paper, do anything to stop the Red Army from reaching the Atlantic whenever the Kremlin might decide to do so. Fortunately, however, police duties in the 'independent' Communist countries of eastern Europe have tied down a heartening number of Soviet divisions ever since 1945.

The postwar Red Army (restyled 'Soviet Army' in March 1946) was not allowed to stagnate: on the contrary, it was promptly reorganized to put a greater emphasis than ever before on the role of armour, and in general to get maximum effectiveness from its frontline strength of 25,000 tanks. Out of the overall strength of 175 divisions, 65 divisions were reformed as mechanized or tank divisions. The new-look Russian mechanized division had a strength of 190 T-34s and self-propelled guns; the new tank division had three T-34 regiments of 200 tanks apiece and a heavy tank regiment with 50 tanks.

Their medium tank remained the superb T-34/85, which might well be described as the 'patron tank' of the Communist world and its allies. The ultimate all-rounder, T-34 has served in sub-zero ice and snow, desert sand, forests, swamps and open country, and street-fighting in all the capitals of eastern Europe. Thirty-six years after its first appearance, it is still a familiar sight on newsreel screens depicting Communist-inspired takeovers in Angola or Beirut. Israeli armoured units have had the most opportunity to appreciate T-34's strengths and weaknesses since 1945, having come up against it in the Middle East wars of 1956, 1967 and 1973. The same applies to T-34's offshoots in the line of self-propelled guns, SU-85 and SU-100.

The T-34 deserves the credit for another achievement, one which never seems to get the publicity it deserves. This achievement has been the amazing speed in which the mechanically retarded Soviet Union, Red China, North Korea and Vietnam have become sophisticated practitioners of mobile warfare. Historians of the future will doubtless moralize over the way in which the Western democracies, sated with mechanical luxuries and private motor transport, compared poorly with the conscript workers and peasants of the Eastern bloc in military efficiency and preparedness. And T-34 was the tank that made the Communist world as strong as it has become in so short a time.

To Western eyes, the Russian use of armour in eastern Europe has been symbolized by the speed with which the tanks went in to put down the East Berlin riots of 1953, the Budapest rising of 1956, and the embarrassing drift to independence shown by the Czechs in 1968: the ultimate expression of alien military supremacy. Against crowds of stone-hurling demonstrators, however incensed the latter may be, a closed-down tank has little to fear providing that the tank commanders stay vigilant and keep each others' machines covered.

1953, 1956, 1968: the brutal punch of the Soviet mailed fist

RIGHT East Berlin, 1953: rioters subdued by T34/85s.

FAR RIGHT Budapest, 1956: exultant Hungarian Freedom Fighters ride a captured T-54.

BELOW Budapest, 1956: another brief gleam of triumph for the Freedom Fighters. The shattered turret lies yards from this gutted T-54.

FAR RIGHT CENTRE Budapest, 1956: the end. Massed T-34s cover every conceivable zone of fire at a crossroads after the crushing of the rising.

ḤT BOTTOM Prague, 1968: a
4 bears down on helpless
onstrators.

T-54: the Russian menace grows

But the fact remains that tanks are always at a fundamental disadvantage when operating in the confines of a city. Home-made missiles and fire bombs can be lobbed down open turrets from upper storeys, and a determined man who keeps his wits, stays out of the field of fire of the machine-guns, and moves fast enough, can get aboard a tank with a petrol bomb. If he is not immediately picked off by covering fire, he has the tank's crew bottled up. Sooner or later they must emerge to tackle him, and if he keeps his head and waits for the first hatch to open he has the chance to destroy the whole crew.

Such a situation implies the existence of an underground resistance army with sufficient training and weapons to wait for its chance. The classic example of what such a resistance army can do against trained regular troops was given by the Warsaw rising of August–October 1944, when the insurgents virtually won control of the whole city on Day One. The German army and SS troops, having roped off the areas of the city under Polish control, were then forced into a replay of Stalingrad: a house-by-house concentric advance, splitting up the defenders, driving them into the open with artillery and flame-throwers. In this fight the spearheads of the Red Army stayed where they were on the far side of the Vistula, declining to enter the battle. Time worked against the Poles, isolated as they were, running ever shorter of ammunition, food, and medical supplies, and not receiving anything like enough from the scanty air drops sent across hundreds of miles of German-occupied territory from the west.

At Warsaw the tank's most valuable role in city fighting was found to be a secondary one. A tank stationed at a street intersection can command one street with its hull machine-guns and the other three with its turret gun and machine-gun. Parked out there in the centre of the crossroads, it is comparatively safe from insurgent missiles and can come closest to fulfilling its true role: inflicting maximum damage with minimum risk to itself. Since 1945 the biggest trouble faced by Russian tanks in this kind of crisis was in Budapest in 1956, and even then the Hungarian Freedom Fighters, for all their gallantry, were nothing like as well armed or prepared as the Poles had been in Warsaw in 1944.

The last Russian heavy of the Second World War, the JS-3, was kept in service well into the 1950s. It set new standards in well-sloped armour (200 mm maximum) and had a low-profile, domed turret carrying a 122-mm gun. If anything, however, the design of JS-3 created as many problems as it solved. Protection was amply provided, but the streamlining and economical lines made it a cramped fighting vehicle for the crew, cut down ammunition stowage, and even – by giving the crew as little possible elbow-room – reduced the rate of fire. The trend of Russian armour since the early 1950s has been to combine, as far as possible, the best qualities of the T-34 medium and the JS-2 and JS-3 heavies. First came an intermediary, experimental machine, T-44, with an 85-mm gun, and then the T-54 (1954), an excellent compromise incorporating many sophistications previously unheard-of in the Soviet tank arm. Compare the following basic specifications from the JS-3 heavy, the T-34/85 and the T-54:

	JS-3	T-34/85	T-54
Weight	46 tons	32 tons	36 tons
Crew	4	4	4
Armament	122-mm + 2 mg	85-mm + 2 mg	100-mm + 2 mg
Armour	200 mm	75 mm	105 mm
Speed	25 mph	31 mph	34 mph

JS-3.

The T-54 proved that the Russians had successfully avoided the temptation to drift into a new breed of ever-slower super-heavy tank – as they had done with the T-35 back in the 1930s, and as the British, Americans and Germans were doing by the end of the Second World War. While losing nothing in streamlining and armoured protection, T-54's flat, domed turret gave the crew far more room, and the tank also adopted the highly-successful 100-mm gun previously used only in self-propelled guns. The T-54 is now the standard Russian 'export', and television viewers will remember having sighted it as far afield as Vietnam, Angola, and the Lebanon (where in November 1976 the Syrian 'peace-keeping force' rolled cautiously into Beirut with their leading T-54s fitted with mine-detonating rollers). T-54 has all the toughness of the T-34 stable, plus far superior electrical traversing gear for the turret and night-fighting aids such as an infra-red 'searchlight' for seeing and shooting in the dark.

T-54's successor has been the T-62, which has improved on the medium-heavy tank compromise. Its silhouette is very similar but it does not have the bracket-mounted machine-gun on the turret and it has a heavier 115-mm gun, recognizable because of the fume extractor halfway down the barrel. This device is a postwar refinement to heavy-calibre tank guns. It is a cylinder sheathing holes drilled in the barrel which prevent fumes being sucked back out of the breech into the crew compartment after each shot. The T-62 has the basic crew of four but it is 6 tons heavier and 6 mph faster than T-54.

ABOVE Lebanon, 1976: a Syrian T-54 crushes a roadblock as the armour of the 'peace-keeping forces' rolls into shattered Beirut.

T-62.

After Sherman, Pershing and Patton: America's M-48

Before the Leopard: the American M-48 in *Bundeswehr* markings.

M-48.

The Western democracies were no more tempted to abandon tank development than the Russians, faced as they were by the largest and most homogeneous tank army on the planet. The Russians, well aware of the individual strengths of Allied tank designs in the Western World, knew very well that agreement on an anti-Soviet joint weapons policy was the biggest potential threat to their military supremacy, which is in itself sufficient explanation for the belligerence and suspicion of postwar Russian diplomacy, replete with accusations of anti-Soviet 'conspiracies'. Unfortunately (or fortunately, depending on your point of view) there has never been any likelihood of such a combination. The politicians and diplomats of the Free World would have managed to prevent such a programme without the monumental influence exerted by the arms manufacturers who have thrived on the cut-throat international market in weapons since 1945. One fact is easy to pin down, however: the end of the Second World War caused far more heart-searching in the Free World over whether or not the tank had a future at all, and tank development in the West suffered accordingly.

One of the most welcome, if unpredictable, features has been the great British resurgence in the field of tank design. British tank development remained depressing and inadequate down to 1944. In the field of medium tanks they had followed up the unsound, under-gunned Crusader with the even more unsound Cavalier and eventually (1944) produced the Cromwell, two years late, given the quality of the opposition. The Cromwell was at least mechanically reliable and had a 75-mm gun that could fire high explosive shells as well as solid shot, but to look at it one would think that sloped armour had never been heard of – all vertical planes and square angles, totally outclassed by the Panther and just about on a par with Germany's ageing Mk IV Specials. Nor could its

ABOVE AND BELOW The Cromwell.

turret take a gun bigger than the 75 mm – another unlearned lesson. The sequel was the mendaciously-named Challenger, a scaled-up Cromwell with a huge, boxy turret enclosing the 76·2-mm gun. The latter at least gave the Challenger gun superiority over the Panther but made Challenger an even better target. The Comet, which just reached the front in time for the last two months of the European war, was much better: sloped turret, reliable and packing a 77-mm gun.

While work was still continuing on the ludicrous Tortoise (see above, p. 106), common sense was at last emerging with a major re-thinking of future tank design in 1944. The result was project A-41 – the Centurion, which anticipated the Russian blend of cruiser and heavy tank by nearly ten years. The Centurion I emerged just too late to cut its teeth in Germany in 1945. It carried the 76·2 mm gun and improved on the good armour standards of Cromwell and Comet, and for the first time ever this new British design incorporated a sloped glacis plate (the upper front shell of the hull). After the ending of hostilities, when the latest German designs could be examined and appraised at leisure, all the combat experience of the Second World War plus the best German ideas were blended to produce Centurion III (1948). It was the best-armoured British tank (152 mm) that had ever been produced; its cross-country performance was good, thanks to wider tracks and improved suspension; the flattish turret made for a low profile; and the brand-new 84-mm gun was fitted with electronic stabilizers that made Centurion III a superb gun platform. Combat experience in Korea and the Middle East showed that it was more than a match for its Russian counterparts.

The Americans ended the war with the M-26 Pershing and spent the next five years ringing the changes on this design. Unlike the British they did not embark

The Comet.

Britain's ageing masterpiece: the superb Chieftain

Fighting profile: a Chieftain shows off its low silhouette and menacing 120-mm gun.

ABOVE The superb Centurion III.

M-60.

on an overhaul of their ideas and produce an equivalent of Centurion, being doubtful of the future role of the tank. The Korean War made them wake up. General MacArthur's push into North Korea was met by the Red Chinese counter-offensive of November 1950, which drove the United Nations forces back into South Korea and took Seoul. Communist-manned T-34/85s were in the forefront of the Red breakthrough and proved conclusively that tanks, once they had broken loose into the enemy's rear, were as great a threat as ever.

In their improved versions of the Pershing design the Americans stuck to the 90-mm gun. The redesigned turret and lower profile of the M-47 Patton reflects the sudden American swing in favour of the tank's anti-tank role; on appearance alone, the Patton looked far more like the Second World War Hellcat tank destroyer than the Pershing or even the Sherman. American failure to develop a high-velocity tank gun of their own had led to the Sherman-Firefly of the Second World War and it remained a persistent weakness after the war. The Patton's successor, the M-60 A-1, used the British 105-mm gun that has been adopted by nearly every armoured force in NATO.

An interesting version of the Patton was the Japanese Type 61 – virtually a carbon copy of the American tank, but using previous Japanese tank experience with controlled differential steering. Smaller in stature than their western counterparts, Japanese tank crewmen have a much easier time of it in the confines of a tank, more room to move always meaning less fatigue and extended endurance.

A common misconception about the international arms trade is that Western machines go to Western client states and Soviet machines to Soviet satellites and client states, with no overlap. But the demarcation is much more blurred than that. A classic example was the Suez crisis and Arab-Israeli War of 1956, remarkable for the first Israeli *blitzkrieg* across the Sinai desert to reach the Suez Canal. The Israelis relied mainly on Shermans and the postwar French light AMX-13, with its 75-mm gun and flimsy armour. The armoured fighting vehicles used by the Egyptian army were a polyglot collection from British, American and Soviet sources, but none the less effective; and the variety of captured Egyptian AFVs in the 1956 Sinai campaign is revealing.

The Israelis only captured 26 T-34s and six SU-100 self-propelled guns, 60 tracked and armoured troop-carriers, and one T-34 command tank. But they took 52 Shermans, one Sherman tank-recoverer and one all-purpose 'tank-dozer' tank recovery vehicle, 260 Bren-gun carriers and 15 unarmed Valentines. The item of Egyptian armour which caused most problems for Israeli tanks was a Second World War throwback, the Archer self-propelled anti-tank gun – a British confection consisting of a 17-pounder mounted backwards on a Valentine hull, introduced in 1943 as a stop-gap measure against the new Panzers. For all its limited traverse and field of fire, the Archer was ideal for use in static positions, which was where the Egyptian troops fought best in 1956. The Archer was a key weapon in the Egyptian anti-tank nests dotting the Sinai and handled the Israeli armour roughly – but the refusal of Egyptian troops to indulge in hand-to-hand combat meant that these anti-tank nests did not hold out against determined attacks, and 40 Archers were captured by the Israelis.

Free World journalists hailed the modern *blitzkrieg,* but in fact the 1956 war was shrouded in dense political overtones. It was the first armoured campaign to be fought with both sides looking over their shoulders, ears straining to catch the shifting nuances of international opinion. There is no indication that David was worrying about what the spectators might think when he went out to tackle Goliath, and certainly fears of what the United States might do did not inhibit Hitler and the German army during the invasion of Russia in 1941. In 1956 the Israelis were not so lucky, and the eagerness of their troops to get into action was a profound embarrassment as well as a source of pride.

Sold to the Egyptians as British war surplus, it gave Israeli armour a tough time in the war of 1956: the Archer self-propelled tank killer.

NATO's dilemma:
West Germany's Leopard 2

Leopard 2 in concealed firing position.

Moshe Dayan's memoir of the war (*Diary of the Sinai Campaign, 1956*) shows that the whole Israeli army – not merely its armoured brigade – was infected with the *blitzkrieg* spirit. He had the sense not to exorcise the latter, and to Guderian's classic maxims, 'Mass, not driblets', and 'Clout 'em, don't tickle 'em', Dayan added, 'Better to be engaged in restraining the noble stallion than in prodding the reluctant mule.' There were many vivid reminders of Guderian's calculated insubordination in 1940; Dayan, writing of the paratroops dropped to block the Mitla Pass on the central axis of the Israeli advance, writes:

> 'The brigade commander had wanted to advance and seize the pass, but there was a specific order from GHQ forbidding this. He therefore requested and received permission to send out a patrol, and towards noon a "patrol unit" set forth. This unit was in fact a full combat team, quite capable of capturing the pass ... the deputy commander of the brigade went along, too.'

All the old lessons of the Second World War were reaffirmed. Air cover and pinpoint attacks from the air were vital; so was the need for proper reconnaissance to prevent tanks from charging blindly to destruction against prepared defences. Minefields proved as big a hazard to tanks as ever. Several times Israeli ground forces were attacked by their own aircraft, an evergreen hazard of modern war. Often this was the fault of the Israelis on the ground, who captured Egyptian tanks and vehicles and pressed them into instant service without identifying them properly as 'ours, not theirs'. And again, despite all its theoretical advantages, the combat value of the light tank (in 1956 France's AMX-13) was found to be severely limited because of its scanty armour. 'Speed is armour', Britain's Admiral Fisher had claimed before 1914, exulting over the new battle-cruisers – but speed is not armour. Three of those battle-cruisers were blown sky-high at Jutland in 1916, and still the myth persisted, with HMS *Hood* following them 25 years later. The light tank is an exact parallel to the battle-cruiser, having a strictly limited role. It must never try to take on opposition tougher than itself or it faces certain destruction.

After 1956 the flow of tanks was intensified from both East and West. The Russians stepped up their supply of armour and other weapons and spares to reinforce Israel's Arab neighbours. British Centurions began to arrive in Israel. The French developed the AMX-30, declining the high-velocity British 105-mm gun for a lower velocity version of their own. The revived German army of 1955, the *Bundeswehr*, came into existence with the old Panzer traditions still very much alive and developed an impressive tank, the Leopard or 'Leo', as it is affectionately known. For Leopard the Germans did take the British gun and have produced one of the best tanks to emerge since the war.

Whatever the eventual verdict on the Leopard may be, it can never be said that it was a hasty or ill-conceived design. Leopard is in fact now (November 1976) one of the top contenders for selection as NATO's main battle tank. There have been 16 prototypes; chassis tests alone have taken four years; engine tests have totalled a gruelling twenty-five weeks. But the Leopard trials form the centrepiece to an Anglo-American-West German wrangle over what is best for NATO's armoured future – and, at the same time, for the armament industries of the three countries involved.

In 1965 Britain introduced Chieftain, the successor to the excellent Centurion. Planned with care and an eye on getting the most long-lived value for taxpayers' money, Chieftain is intended to be the main British battle tank until the 1980s. All the best features were taken from Centurion and added to a new 50-ton tank with the emphasis on armoured protection and the excellent hitting-power of Britain's new 120-mm gun. All these features were achieved in a tank with an admirably low profile, yet without unduly cramped crew accommodation.

Chieftain became the running mate of the American M-48s which equipped West Germany's Panzer forces during the development of Leopard, and the

ABOVE Typical of NATO disagreements: the impressive MBT (Main Battle Tank) 70 of the late 1960s. It started life as an American–German exercise but the two sides fell out over armament. The Americans favoured a gun-missile system, the Shillelagh; the Germans wanted a high-velocity gun. The debate continues.

RIGHT Germany's Leopard 2 on its gruelling trials, using a stream bed in time-honoured Panzer style.

AMX-30.

Britain's nuclear-age tank, the Chieftain, on exercises with the Rhine Army in Germany.

US army's M-60s. The trouble started in 1971 when the Americans started to look for a replacement for the M-60, and national weapons industries almost immediately rivalled strategic requirements in importance.

The new American project was christened XM-1, and the first need was to agree on its gun. The standard NATO tank gun (fitted in 9000 NATO tanks) was still the British 105 mm, but everyone was now looking for a tank gun with greater hitting-power. For XM-1 and the Leopard 2, America and West Germany agreed to standardize equipment. Trials were held to select the best gun – the old British 105 mm, the new British 110 mm and the German 120 mm, the latter a smoothbore gun firing a dart-like fin-stabilized missile. Both sides claimed victory in the tests at Shoeburyness in August 1975. The British 105 mm was edged out of the running by its lower hitting power; the German 120 mm was best for range and penetration and the British 110 mm for accuracy. One thing was clear: Britain was falling behind in the race to produce an improved 120-mm gun that would outdo the German equivalent.

Apart from the furore over Britain's revolutionary new 'Chobham armour' (see below, p. 134), another source of discord emerged between the Germans and the Americans over the trials of Leopard. West Germany naturally held out hopes that Leopard 2 would be selected as the main NATO battle tank, but the Americans continue to criticize its suspension and cross-country performance. The harder suspension favoured by the Germans to provide a solid gun platform certainly makes for a rougher cross-country ride for the crew; Americans prefer a softer ride, cutting down on crew fatigue and accepting the risk that a deeper suspension (causing greater recoil when the gun is fired) may effect accuracy when in rapid fire. Champions of the Leopard point out that it has an American fire-control sub-system anyway; and one Panzer officer's viewpoint, quoted by Tony Geraghty of *The Sunday Times,* harks back to the eternal fact that tank designers can never win. 'You can have your soft ride and be dead pretty soon, or shoot straight and survive, even if you get a little stiff in the process.'

The debate continues at the time of going to press. Britain's Chieftain is scheduled for phasing-out in the 1980s and its replacement will be an improved Super-Chieftain unless the Anglo-American contest is satisfactorily resolved. A long-term project for an Anglo-German tank has yet to bear fruit. That it will have taken some twenty years to produce a new battle tank for NATO is a frightening commentary on the prospects of the Free World – the stakes are so much higher than the money to be made by the arms industries of the three countries involved. Communists may jeer at the impotence and fundamental malaise and greed of the capitalist world, yet they know that the men who would man the tanks on the Soviet side for the unimagineable showdown in Europe's last battle would be up against the finest military technology that money and brainpower can produce. A camel may be 'a horse designed by a committee', but joint research and know-how has produced quite as many excellent tanks as it has failures.

the Nuclear Age

Over sixty years have passed since the tank made its debut on the Somme in the First World War, and the tank is still with us. It has defied innumerable prophecies that such-and-such a weapon would make it redundant, and seems certain to go on doing so because no better expedient has been found for protecting soldiers on the battle-field and concentrating their fighting capacity into an overwhelming force.

One eternal factor in the story of the tank has been the application of technology and ballistics to the escalation problem. Side A must have a tank that must stand up to the fire of Side B's tank and overcome Side B's tank with its own hitting-power. As soon as Side B produces a better tank, Side A must be ready to produce one that is better still.

Another fundamental truth about tanks is that every single advantage which can be built into a tank has a twin disadvantage, and that every tank is a compromise because of this. A balance sheet of tank pros and cons works out something like this:

Good	Bad
Heavy armour	Weight
Big gun	Bigger turret, bigger target
Speed	Lightweight armour, lower hitting-power
Low profile in fire position	Less room for crew, more fatigue
Comfortable crew accommodation	Bigger tank, bigger target
Deep suspension, comfortable for crew	More recoil, less accuracy
Hard suspension, better for accuracy	Rougher on crews, cuts down endurance
Long range	Bigger fuel tanks and fire risk or Heavier armour for tanks, more deadweight

A good example of these pros and cons at work today may be found in the story of Britain's Chobham armour (named after the home of the Military Vehicles and Engineering Establishment at Chobham, Surrey, where it was developed in the late 1960s). Chobham armour is an undoubted technical breakthrough. It is not a solid steel plate but a shock-absorbing sponge, giving three times the protection of traditional armour for no extra weight. It can handle orthodox solid shot or hollow-charge HEAT (High Explosive Anti-Tank), and it is said to put little on the price of a brand-new tank. The Chieftain tanks sold to Iran will have the Chobham armour and details of Chobham have been passed to the United States and to West Germany. It is excellent news for NATO – but it will only be a matter of time before a new anti-tank missile is perfected to cope with it.

The Chobham story has an embarrassing twist to it. Nothing shows better how far Britain has come from the rock-bottom of tank technology in the Second World War. By promptly passing on the new invention to her allies, keeping faith with them, Britain has made a heartening contribution to the security of

PREVIOUS PAGES The year is 1965, but these Soviet T-54s tackle a water obstacle in the same way as the trail-blazing British tanks at Cambrai in 1917: once across, a sharp right-angled turn to mop up defenders. Soviet Russia continues to add to the strongest tank army in the world; its training continues. Training for what?

the Free World. But already the detractors and complicators are at work, busily running down what they condemn as a naïve giving-away of a priceless asset worth millions of pounds *and getting nothing in return*. One British general was quoted as saying that the British had been 'boy scouts' in the affair, and it was time they grew up. Considering the speed at which the Soviet build-up of military might continues in the late 1970s, the fact that Britain was short of money might have been considered of slightly less importance than making a priceless contribution to the world military balance.

Whatever the financial rights and wrongs underlying Britain's announcement of Chobham armour, the essential point is that it is a temporary phenomenon. Sooner or later, it is going to be overmatched by a superior projectile.

Apart from the gun, what other conventional weapons are the modern tank's worst enemies?

The Middle East wars have proved that the old-fashioned minefield is as dangerous as ever. Specialized armour remains the only way to tackle a minefield with reasonable speed; but it is easy to plant a dummy minefield which registers convincingly on mine-detectors. Although ostentatious mine-clearing activities do not always herald a *bona fide* assault – by indicating a feint, such activities are an important part of tactical bluff and double-bluff – the fact remains that it is suicide to send a tank attack into a minefield without clearing gaps first.

Obstacles are another story. Nearly every modern battle tank is equipped to wade rivers, its engine breathing through a schnorkel tube – but wading tanks are no use when the 'enemy' bank of the river to be crossed is too steep to allow them to crawl ashore. Gapping and bridging armoured fighting vehicles have survived, the heirs of the Normandy Funnies. Nearly every artificial obstacle can be artificially circumvented.

Israeli 'Super Shermans' on the Golan Heights in the 1967 'Six Day War'. After the desert war in North Africa between 1940 and 1943, the Middle East wars of 1956, 1967 and 1973 have proved that desert warfare still offers ideal scope for massed armour.

Specialized armour of the 1970s: a
Chieftain bridge-layer. 'Nearly every
artificial obstacle can be artificially
circumvented.'

Rocket missiles are the last in the line of devices supposed to make the tank
redundant. The first unguided anti-tank missiles used in the Second World
War did give a single infantryman the chance to knock out a tank, but they were
not infallible. The hollow-charge warhead had to strike squarely to achieve full
penetration; even when it did, there were miraculous cases of crews surviving
the blast. Above all, the rocketeer only got one chance at dangerously short
range – under 100 yards.

The guided missile was another proposition, delivering as it does a larger
missile over a longer range – a missile that can be steered to its target. Here the
trouble is the equipment needed to get a missile on its way and delivered
accurately to its target: power supply, missile selection box, generation box,
control stick and optical sight. The first guided missiles were wire-guided,
paying out a length of wire in flight to transmit the operator's signals – another
complication. The anti-tank guided missile trend was obvious: a search for a
small rocket and economic launch-and-guidance pack that could be carried
and operated by one man. A typical example, which emerged in the 1960s, is
Sweden's BANTAM – the Bofors Anti-Tank Missile. BANTAM's carrying
container is also its launch pad, a box seven inches square and just over a yard
long that can be slung on a man's back or carried like an ammunition box.

BANTAM is certainly one of the most compact anti-tank missiles in service
in the 1970s. The missile's fins expand in flight; it can be mounted in batteries
on light vehicles or infantry handcarts; it can be concealed in soil, snow or
loose rocks. The warhead is a double-shelled hollow charge designed to ignite
on hitting any object, even at angles of less than ten degrees; it penetrates over
500 mm of solid armour plate and is effective up to 2000 metres. As an additional
bonus, BANTAM is designed to work in temperatures down to −40°C. and
up to +60°C.

In short, BANTAM would appear to be the ultimate answer to any tank
foolish enough to venture within 2000 metres' range: marvellously compact,
long-ranging and hard-hitting. All this is true – but it still takes at least half a
minute from carrying to firing – 30–50 seconds is the time quoted in BANTAM's
promotional literature. And in 30–50 seconds a lot of extremely unpleasant
things can happen on a battlefield. The full sequence for preparing BANTAM
to kill a tank is as follows:

Despite the gloomiest forecasts of the pundits, increasingly sophisticated anti-tank missiles – this is a Swingfire, launched from a Ferret scout car – have not yet succeeded in bringing about the demise of the tank.

Missile preparation
Down container;
Rear cover off, rear edge of container elevated;
Front cover off, control cable connected.

Control unit preparation
Support legs unfolded, control unit on ground;
Connect cable;
Cover off;
Fold up sight;
Push test button for functioning check;
Safety release off, system ready to fire.

Now this sounds like a very straightforward, simple sequence until the conditions of battle are added – artillery bombardment, enemy air strikes, small-arms fire from infiltrating infantry. Obviously BANTAM is best suited for firing from prepared anti-tank sites without such harassment, which limits its employment considerably and gives the approaching tank much more of a chance.

A tremendous impact was made during the opening phase of the Yom Kippur War of October 1973, when Egyptian infantrymen swarmed across the Suez Canal in rubber dinghies, deployed their Soviet SAGGER missiles, and knocked out 100 Israeli tanks as they moved rashly in to counter-attack. But just because the Egyptians had gained virtually total surprise due to Israeli negligence, and because clumsy Israeli tactics gave the Egyptian missile men ideal conditions on a plate, this did not mean that the SAGGER was in itself the answer to the tank. It certainly did not win the war: once the Israelis had pulled themselves together they bided their time until the Egyptians were at full strength, then launched a classic 'revolving door' offensive westward across the canal, menaced the Egyptian supply artery and executed a perfect 'pincer-and-pocket' trapping move at Suez, negating nearly all the initial Egyptian gains at a stroke.

Perhaps the Yom Kippur War will stand as the perfect allegory of the correct role of the tank in the missile age. Nothing has changed. Expose tanks to specialized anti-tank weapons on ground of the latter's choosing and the result must be disaster for the tanks; use tanks as they should be used, as a scalpel to sever the enemy's tendons, and at the very least you will impose a tactical stalemate, if not 'peace with honour' or outright victory.

If the postwar Middle East campaigns have proved an orthodox testing-ground for modern armour, the Communist conquest of South Vietnam saw the tank used in its most unorthodox role to date.

The problem facing the Vietcong for the bulk of the war was how to stay alive and keep operating in the south, given the absolute superiority of the US and South Vietnamese forces. The latter held all the cards – not just firepower but mobility as well. Giap, North Vietnam's strategic mastermind, was the first outgunned commander ever to look over the heads of the military opposition to the enemy civilian population and gamble, successfully, that America's heart was not in the war. After three years' ordeal the Vietcong were still there. Then came the key year of 1968. Giap's stunning Tet offensive won no vital military objectives but it shattered dwindling American hopes that the Vietcong was being worn down to breaking point.

Not until the initiative had clearly shifted in his favour did Giap turn his whole strategy upside down and place the emphasis on *regular* military operations to generate more *guerrilla* operations. He opened the armoury which had been impressively stocked by the Russians: heavy artillery to match that of the American forces, and above all T-54 tanks. Vietnam was not tank country – on the contrary, the terrain offered splendid opportunities for tank hunting. The guns and the T-54s which rolled remorselessly into Saigon were not instruments of victory, but symbols of victory. Instead of winning the war for the Vietcong, the tanks, when they appeared for the last act, *proved the war had been won.* For the crumbling remnants of South Vietnamese resistance it was the last straw: fruitless years of chasing invisible guerrillas, only to have them turn into armoured units and attack in greater strength than ever.

In a sense, of course, the tank has always traded heavily on its looks: evil, impersonal, the epitome of irresistible power and crushing weight. This aura of power lends itself superbly to propaganda and totalitarianism, a comforting

Vietnam, 1975, the nearest we have come to seeing a modern revolution in tank strategy. The North Vietnamese did not unleash their Soviet-supplied tanks *until* they had won the upper hand in the long guerrilla war – the tank employed as the proof and symbol of victory already won.

August 1976. 'Somewhere in eastern
Europe' massed Soviet T-62s continue to
train with chilling efficiency. The
nightmare the West chooses to forget –
this could be the Rhine.

fillip for Western morale: it is the Hitlers, Stalins and Krushchevs who like to
stand on saluting-points watching massed columns of tanks stream by. Nor
was Giap the first leader to build up a modern armoured army from guerrilla
origins – Tito had done it in Yugoslavia during the Second World War, and
Mao Tse-tung in the Chinese Civil War of 1946–9. Both Tito and Mao, needless
to say, had got their tanks from Russia. But never in the tank's six decades of
operational existence has it been used in the way Giap's men used it: as armour-
plated proof of victory *after* the back of enemy resistance had been broken by
the persistence of guerrillas.

What, if anything, can be said to justify the tank's existence in nuclear war?

It is now accepted that everything at 'ground centre' of a nuclear blast is
destroyed, with the likelihood of survival increasing the further away from the
centre you happen to be. The terrible effects of nuclear explosions come from
three main by-products: heat, blast and radiation. Men in an armoured vehicle
have a far better chance of surviving the heat and blast; the biggest danger is
the radiation. When we finally learn to make tanks completely self-supporting,
producing their own air and recycling water, the traditional taunt that of course
tanks would be useless in a nuclear war will no longer be true.

The mind does boggle at the thought of a combat vehicle on the lines of an
armoured fighting space capsule, but the scientific pace of this century has
made it unwise to mock too loudly or too soon. Sixty years ago it was all a tank
could do to cross an 8-foot trench, and it is only thirty-six years ago since it was
proved that tanks can be sealed watertight and crawl across the sea bed. A
radiation-proof tank is by no means a pipe-dream for the future.

But what purpose could a radiation-proof tank possibly serve in a seared and
contaminated world? To this there is no answer. The tank is an instrument to
enable men to survive an impossible environment; to carry them, as the colours
of the original British Tank Corps suggested, 'From Mud Through Blood to
the Green Fields Beyond'. Whether or not those fields will be hopelessly
radioactive will be for men to decide.

Appendices

I Guns, calibres, shot and shell

The size of a tank's gun is nowadays classified by its **calibre**, the internal diameter of the barrel, measured in millimetres. Thus a 128-mm shell is 128 mm thick (not long) – just over 5 inches and about the size fired by the main guns of a naval destroyer.

A good tank gun must be able to fire a variety of projectiles: **high explosive** against enemy infantry or defences, **anti-tank** solid shot or explosive shell for fighting other tanks, **smoke** shells, etc. A tank which surprises a column of enemy trucks would probably use high explosive, saving its specialized anti-tank projectiles (old-fashioned solid shot could easily go right through a truck without destroying it or even setting it on fire).

The longer the range and the more devastating the hit required, the higher the gun's **velocity** must be. This can be achieved by accelerating the projectile. The tighter the squeeze and the longer the travel down the barrel, the faster the projectile will go. Many experiments have been made in increasing the barrel squeeze and the 'popgun' effect as the shell leaves the muzzle. Projectiles were fitted with collar-like **sabots** which fell off on leaving the muzzle; or given extra-hard cores and soft-metal outer skins intended to be scoured off in the barrel. In the Second World War the Germans came up with the 'squeeze gun', 28 mm at the breech and 20 mm at the muzzle. This gave a muzzle velocity of 4600 feet per second – satisfactorily high, but very rough on the life of the gun, and it also meant making special tungsten-cored shells which could stand up to it. Germany never had enough tungsten anyway. Another squeeze device, the British Littlejohn adaptor, was simply fixed to the end of the muzzle. But the basic expedient of scaling-up the calibre to 100 mm plus has proved the most effective way of increasing the range and punch of tank guns.

Not content with driving on the left, the British also clung to their inches and complicated matters further by taking the **weight** (in pounds) of the projectile. This lasted until the American Stuarts, Grants and Shermans came along in the Second World War with their 37-mm and 75-mm guns and the British finally adopted the metric system for calibres.

Sorting out the weights and measures caused by this intransigence can be confusing, so some comparisons are given here. The 2-pounder gun with which the British tank and anti-tank gunners went to war in 1939 had a calibre of 40 mm, nominally superior to the German 37 mm but inferior in that the 37 mm could fire high explosive as well as solid shot. The 6-pounder was 57 mm, the 17-pounder 76·2 mm (the calibre selected as the basic calibre for the Red Army and the original gun of the T-34), and that versatile British field gun, the 25-pounder gun-howitzer, was 88 mm.

A **gun** uses **direct fire**, hurling its projectile straight at the target in as flat a trajectory as possible. A **howitzer**, using **indirect fire**, lobs its projectile high in the air and is therefore useful for shelling targets on the other sides of hills. Spiral grooves or **rifling** in the barrel spins the projectile while still in the barrel and makes for greater stability and accuracy. Rifling is not required for the humble **mortar**, a simple tube launcher for throwing bombs by indirect fire.

On p. 68 reference is made to the '50-mm L60' and the '50-mm L42'. In this case the terminal figure gives the ratio of calibre to **barrel length**. Thus the 50-mm L60 had a barrel length of 60 × 50 mm, or 3 metres.

A tank's **machine-guns** are intended primarily for use against enemy infantry, but they have another function: as 'sighters' for the main gun. **Tracer**

bullets leave smoke trails by day and luminous streaks by night; the gunner can therefore see where his bullets are going and home in on his target. When the fire of the **co-axial machine-gun** (the one mounted on the same axis as the tank's main gun) is hitting the target, the main gun will too.

Modern stabilizing devices help a tank fire on the move with a modicum of accuracy, but it is always better to halt to fire, the driver moving off as soon as he hears the gun fire. The best motto is to keep moving: an immobile tank's crew feels naked.

II Some tank terms and simple tactics

A tank's **hull** is the main body which carries the revolving **turret**. This can **traverse** through 360°, the hallmark of the true tank. A **self-propelled gun**, although tracked and armoured, has no turret: its gun, mounted in the hull, points forward but only has a very limited traverse. Early British tanks carried their guns in **sponsons**, fixed boxes jutting out from the sides of the tank.

The **glacis plate** is the armoured upper nose of the tank. It is normally sloped to throw off shot. As it is likely to take a good deal of punishment its armour must be thick, and the same applies to the **turret front** and **mantlet**, the plate shielding the gun-mounting.

Spaced armour is like the double skin of a ship and serves the same purpose: to give the machine's vitals maximum protection against forcible arrivals from outside.

Sloped armour, when angled at 50° to the angle of attack, doubles the protection without needing thicker or heavier armour. But if sloped excessively it will mean less room and more fatigue for the crew.

Face-hardened armour is tougher on one side (the outside) than on the other: it was an early stage in the shot-versus-armour escalation contest, causing simple solid shot to break up on impact.

Splash means the molten or white-hot bits of metal hurled off the inside of a tank's armour by hits on the outside. It can maim or kill, particularly (as with early tanks) if a complete rivet is smashed loose.

A **laager** or **leaguer** is a defensive position, normally for a night halt, with all tanks on the outside (like a circle of covered wagons in a Western) for maximum security.

Soft-skinned vehicles, which normally means trucks or lorries, is the term for anything on wheels without armour.

Panzer is not German for 'tank' but 'armour'; it was adopted as the normal word for 'tank' in the late 1930s. PAK (**panzer-abwehr-kanone**) is the German abbreviation for 'anti-tank gun'. Oddly enough, unlike the more well-known FLAK (**flieger-abwehr-kanone**, or 'anti-aircraft gun'), PAK never caught on as part of the Allies' vocabulary.

Normally enemy tanks in the vicinity are reported by reconnaissance armoured cars and light tanks, or from the air. The commander, facing the situation and weighing up the odds, must remember his own objective. Unless he is on his own he may decide simply to duck around the opposition and keep going; he may decide to half-circle and catch the enemy in flank – or he may be grossly outnumbered and forced to fight willy-nilly.

If there are anti-tank gun positions in the area he may be able to lure the enemy tanks within the gunners' range. If time and terrain permit he may decide to lay an ambush, ordering his own tanks into concealment – behind hedgerows, backed into spinneys, shielded by buildings. A tank reversed directly into a building through a wall can be quite invisible apart from its gun muzzle – but the hole it makes will stand out a mile unless the whole area is covered with bomb or shell damage.

In open country a commander will order his tanks to take advantage of whatever ridges and hollows exist, taking up either the **hull-down** position (with only the turret visible to the enemy) or **turret-down**, with the whole tank concealed. It frequently happens that the target is too high or too low for the gun to reach it at full elevation or depression; the commander must then tell his driver to use nearby slopes so that the gun can be brought on target.

Tanks can be disguised as trucks by canvas screens which can be discarded in an instant. A small tank force in dusty or desert terrain can look like a whole army by trailing objects to throw up dust. Campaigning in winter means keeping an eye open for possible snow and keeping the whitewash handy, for uncamouflaged tanks make beautiful targets against newly-fallen snow.

Further Reading

Churchill, Winston, *The World Crisis* (Macmillan 1931).

Clark, Alan, *Barbarossa* (Hutchinson 1965).

Crisp, Robert, *Brazen Chariots* (Frederick Muller 1959; Corgi 1960, 1966).

Dayan, Moshe, *Diary of the Sinai Campaign 1956* (Weidenfeld and Nicolson 1966; Sphere Books 1967).

de Gaulle, Charles, *The Army of the Future* (Levrault 1934).

Guderian, Heinz, *Panzer Leader* (Michael Joseph 1952; Futura Publications 1974).

Liddell Hart, Basil, *The Rommel Papers* (Collins 1953). *The Tanks,* 2 vols (Cassell 1959).

Mackintosh, Malcolm, *Juggernaut* (Secker and Warburg 1967).

Macksey, Kenneth, *To the Green Fields Beyond* (published privately by Regimental Headquarters, Royal Tank Regiment 1965). *Armoured Crusader* (Hutchinson 1967). *The Shadow of Vimy Ridge* (Kimber 1965). *Afrika Corps* (Pan/Ballantine 1968). *Panzer Division* (Pan/Ballantine 1968).

Macksey, Kenneth, and Batchelor, John, *Tank : A History of the Armoured Fighting Vehicle* (BPC/Ballantine, 1971).

Mellenthin, F.W.von, *Panzer Battles* (Cassell 1955; University of Oklahoma Press 1956).

Orgill, Douglas, *T34 : Russian Armour* (Pan/Ballantine 1971).

Ogorkiewicz, R.M. *Armour* (Stevens 1959). *The Design and Development of Fighting Vehicles* (Macdonald 1968).

Stern, A., *Log Book of a Pioneer* (Hodder and Stoughton 1919).

Swinton, E., *Eyewitness* (Hodder and Stoughton 1932).

History of the First World War, 8 vols (Purnell).

History of the Second World War, 8 vols (Purnell).

World War II, 8 vols (Orbis Books).

World War II Tanks (Orbis Books).

Index

Afrika Korps, 72–3, 86, 97
Aisne R., 64
Alamein, battle of, 86, 101
Amiens, battle of, 33
Angola, 117
Arab–Israeli War (1956), 125
Ardennes (1944), 105
armour and shot, 27, 59, 63, 84–6, 89, 134–5, 140–2
armoured cars, 13, 58, 141
Arnim, General Jürgen von, 97
Arras (1917), 18, 27, 30
Arras (1940), 63
Asquith, Herbert, Prime Minister, 20
Aubers Ridge, 19

Bacon, Sir Reginald, Admiral, 19–20
Balkan campaign (1941), 73, 76
BANTAM, 136–7
Bapaume, 31
'Barbarossa', 76–7
Batter, F. W., 13
Battle of Britain, 68
'Battleaxe', 76
bazooka, 103
Beck, General Ludwig, 52
Beda Fomm, 69, 72
Beirut, 117
Belgium, 18, 62
Benghazi, 73
Benz, Karl, 13
Berlin, battle of, 102
Bialystok, 81
'Big Willie', see 'Mother'
Bizerta, 97
Boer War, 8
Bohemia, 9
Bougainville, 88
Budapest rising (1956), 112, 116
Bullock track, 22
'Bullshorn plough', 101
Bundeswehr, 128
Burma, 88

Caen, 103
Cambrai, battle of, 29, 31, 33
Carden-Loyd designs, 41, 44, 51–2, 59
Caucasus, 81, 109
Chemin des Dames, 27, 29
Cherbourg, 64
China, 88, 112, 139
Chobham armour, 131, 134–5
Christie, J. Walter, 51, 58–9
Churchill, Winston S., 8, 19, 20–1, 73, 76, 102
'Citadel', 94–6
Civil War, American, 17
Civil War, Spanish, 45, 55
Courcelette, 25
Courseulles, 101
Coventry Ordnance Works, 19
Cowan, James, 10–11
Crete, 76
Crimean War, 10–11

'Crusader', 85, 107
Czechoslovakia, 55

Daimler, Gottlieb, 13
DAK, *see Afrika Korps*
Dardanelles, 21
d'Eyncourt, Eustace Tennyson, 20–1
Dayan, General Moshe, 128
Diary of the Syrian Campaign, 128
Dieppe, 98
Diplock, Bramah, 11, 13
Donoghue, Major, 13
Dunkirk, 19, 63–4, 68–9

East Berlin riots (1953), 112
East Prussia, 18
Edwards, G. M., 13
Egypt, 69, 86
Eisenhower, General Dwight D., 102
Elles, General Hugh, 22, 29, 59
Estienne, Colonel J. E., 27

Festubert, 19
First World War, development and use of tanks in, 15, 18–33, 40, 45
Flers, 25
Foch, Marshal Ferdinand, 33
For Whom the Bell Tolls, 45
Fosters, 21–2
France: severe infantry losses of, 18–25; development of tanks by, 27; postwar 'cavalry mania' in, 40–1; conquest of, 1940, 62–4, 68; postwar tanks of, 128
Fritsch, General Freiherr von, 52
Fuller, Lieutenant-Colonel J. F. C., 29, 40, 44
'Funnies', *see* tanks, development of specialized

Gamelin, General Maurice, 64
Gatling gun, 9, 12
Gaza, 29
Gazala, 86, 107
Germany: First World War tanks of, 30–1; restrictions of Versailles Treaty on, 50; postwar tank experiments of, 50–1; develops Panzer divisions, 51–2, 55; low tank production of, in Second World War, 68, 81; tank production of, at peak, 104; and Leopard tank, 128–39 *passim*
Giap, General, 138–9
Greece, 73, 76
Guam, 88
Guderian, General Heinz: early theories of, 51–2, 55; in Poland, 61–2; in West, 63–4; Inspector of Armoured Troops, 94, 104, 107; and *Maus*, 106

Haig, Field-Marshal Sir Douglas, 22, 25, 29, 44
Hankey, Colonel Maurice, 20

Hastie, Lieutenant Stuart, 25
Hatfield Park trials, 22
Hemingway, Ernest, 45
Hetherington, Major, 20–1
Hetherington 'Big Wheel', 20–1
'Hindenburg line' (*Siegfried-stellung*), 27, 29, 33
Hitler, Adolf: becomes Chancellor, 51; encourages Panzer development, 51–2; weakens Panzer strength, 68–9; sends *Afrika Korps*, 72–3; ignores Panzer experts, 76, 81, 94; insists on Kursk attack, 94; enthusiasm of, for *Maus*, 106; and defeat of Panzers, 107
Hobart, Major-General Sir Percy, 101–2
Holland, 62
Holt & Co, 13, 22
Hornsby & Co, 13
Hussite Wars, 9–10

Imphal, 88

Kasserine Pass, 97
Kazan, 50–1
Kiev, 76, 81
Killen-Strait tractor, 22
Kitchener, Field-Marshal Lord, 20, 23
Kleist, Field-Marshal Ewald von, 109
Kohima, 88
Korea, 112, 121
Koshkin, Mikhail Ilyich, 61
Kursk salient, 94–7

Land Ironclads, The, 8, 12
Landships Committee of the Admiralty, 20–1
Le Cateau, 18
League of Nations, 58
Lebanon, 117
Lend-Lease, 85
Leningrad, 76
Libya, 69
Liddell Hart, Basil, 51
Liège, 19
Lille, 19
'Little Willie' (Tritton No. 1), 22, 25
Loos, battle of, 19, 25
Lorraine, French defeats in (1914), 18
'Ludendorff offensive' (1918), 30
Luftwaffe, 52, 55, 68, 102, 107
Lutz, Colonel, 51
Luzon, 88

MacArthur, General Douglas, 124
machine-gun, 12, 18, 89
machine-gun carriers, types of: Bren Mk 1, 44, 69; UE, 44; CV-33/35, 44, 69; T-27, 44; TK-3, 44, 61; Skoda MU-4, 44
Mandalay, 88
Manstein, Field-Marshal Erich von, 94

Marne, first battle of, 18
Martel, Major Giffard, 41
Masurian Lakes, 18
Maxim gun, 12–13
Medenine, 97
Meiktila, 88
Meuse R., 63, 76
mines and minesweeping tanks, 96, 101–2, 117, 128, 135; anti-tank, 103
Minsk, 81
Mitchell, Lieutenant F., 31
Mons, battle of, 18, 33
Monte Cassino, 109
Montgomery, Field-Marshal Sir B. L., 86, 97, 103
Morris, William, 41
Mortimore, Lieutenant M. W., 25
Moscow, 76, 81, 94, 104
'Mother' ('Big Willie'), 22–3, 27

Namur, 19
Neuve Chapelle, 19–20
Normandy, 94, 101–3
North African campaign, 69–76, 85–6, 96–7
Norwegian campaign, 62

OKW, 68

Panzer divisions: formation of, 52, 55, 58; in Poland, 61–2; in West (1940), 62–8; Hitler weakens, 68–9; in Balkans, 76; and 'Barbarossa', 76, 81; Guderian reforms, 94; in Normandy, 103; peak tank production for, 104; reasons for defeat of, 107–9
Panzerfaust, 103
Panzerschreck, 103
'Paschendael' ('Third Ypres'), 29
Patton, General George, 103
Pearl Harbor, 85
pedrails, 11–13
PIAT ('Projectile Infantry Anti-Tank') gun, 103
'Plan 1919', 40, 44
Polish campaign, 61–2
Prague (1968), 112
Putlos trials, 68

Rapallo, Treaty of, 50
Red Army, 61, 76, 81, 89–91, 94, 96, 102; postwar strength of, 112–39 *passim*
Reichenau, Field-Marshal von, 51
rocket missiles, anti-tank, 103, 136–7
Rommel, Field-Marshal Erwin: with 7th Panzer, 63–4; first desert campaign of, 72–3; wins 'Battleaxe', 76; and 'Crusader', 76, 107; tank strength of, at Alamein, 86; in Tunisia, 97; in Normandy, 101
Royal Tank Regiment, 31
Rudel, Hans-Ulrich, 96

St Quentin, 31
St Valery, 64
SAGGER, 137
Saigon, 138
Saipan, 88
'Sea Lion', 68
Sedan, 62
self-propelled (SP) guns, 68, 89, 90–1, 94, 105–7
Seoul, 124
Shoeburyness trials (1975), 131
Sidi Barrani, 69
Simms, F. R., 13
Smolensk, 102
Somme, battle of, 25, 31
Somme R., 64
Speer, Albert, 104
Stalin, Josef, 61
Stalingrad, battle of, 81, 94, 104
Steiner, Herr, 13
Stern, Lieutenant Albert, 21, 23
Strand Magazine, The, 8
Stülpnagel, General von, 52
Suez (1956), 125
Swinton, Colonel E. D., 20–1, 23

tanks: medieval origins of, 8–10; steam age designs anticipating, 10–12; first petrol-engined attempts at, 13; demands of First World War to produce, 15, 18–23; first combat use of, 25; developed in France, 27; first massed use of, 29; first tank-v-tank battle, 31; beset by postwar 'cavalry mania', 44–5; Weygand discovers defence against massed, 64; dominance of Soviet, since Second World War, 84; development of specialized, 98–102, 135; and air power, 96, 102, 109, 128; breakthrough tactics of Russian, 102; basic principles for success of, 108–9, 134; weakness of, in street fighting, 81, 112, 116; hampered by politics in 1956, 125–6; NATO versus Warsaw Pact, 112–31; revolutionary use of, in Vietnam, 138–9; future for, 134–9; terminology and basic tactics, 140–2

tanks, types of, American: Christie cruiser, 51, 84; M2A1, 84; M3A Stuart (Honey), 85–6, 88; M3 Lee/Grant, 85–6, 88–9, 98; M4 Sherman, 84, 86, 88–90, 109, 125; Sherman DD, 101; Sherman Crab, 101; Sherman hedgecutter, 102; Sherman Firefly, 105, 109; M26 Pershing, 105, 121, 124; M–47 Patton, 124; M–48, 128; M–60 A1, 124, 130; XM–1, 130
–, British: Tank Mk I/II, 23–7; Mk IV, 29; Mk V, 31, 33; Whippet, 29, 30–1, 33, 46; Vickers Medium II, 40; Vickers Medium C, 40; D, 40; Infantry Mk I, 59; Mk II Matilda, 59, 63, 69; Cruiser A–9, 59, 69; Vickers Light Mk VI, 59, 69; Cruiser A–13, 69; Crusader, 69, 86, 120; Valentine, 69, 86, 98, 101; Churchill, 98, 101; Churchill Ark, 101; Churchill AVRE, 101; Churchill Bobbin, 101; Churchill Crocodile, 101; Cavalier, 120; Cromwell, 120; Challenger, 121; Comet, 121; Centurion, 121, 124; Chieftain, 128, 131, 134
–, French: Schneider CA1, 27, 30; St Chamond, 27, 30; Renault M–17, 30, 40–1; Char-B, 40–1, 52, 59, 63, 68, 86, 98; Renault R–35, 40, 59, 68; Hotchkiss H–35, 40–1, 59, 68; SOMUA S–35, 59; AMX–13, 128; AMX–30, 128
–, German: A7 V, 30, 31; LK II, 33, 50; *Leichte Traktor*, 40, 50; *Grossetraktor*, 50, 52; PzKpfw V, 52; PzKpfw I, 52, 58, 64; PzKpfw II, 52, 55, 58, 64, 86; Pzkpfw III, 52, 55, 58, 64, 68–9, 86, 94, 107; PzKpfw IV, 52, 55, 58, 64, 68–9, 76–7, 86, 94, 107, 120; PzKpfw 35t, 55, 68; PzKpfw 38t, 68–9; PzKpfw V Panther, 84, 94, 103, 105, 107, 120; PzKpfw VI Tiger I, 84, 94, 97–8, 103, 107; Tiger II ('King Tiger'), 84, 104–5; *Maus*, 106; Leopard 2, 128, 130–1
–, Italian: M11/39, 69
–, Japanese: Chi-ha, 88; Type 61, 124
–, Polish: 7TP, 40, 61
–, Russian: 'Lenin', 30; T–26A, 40, 61; T–35, 61; BT series, 51, 61; T–28, 61; T–34/76, 61, 81, 84, 89–90, 94, 107; KV 1, 61, 84, 90, 107; T–34/85, 84, 90, 102, 116, 125; JS–2, 84, 90, 116; JS–3, 90, 116; T–54, 116–17, 138; T–62, 117
Tank–busting aircraft, 96
Tank Corps, 29, 139
Tannenberg, battle of, 18
Thoma, General von, 51
'Tiger Convoy', 76
Tito, Marshal Josip, 139
Tobruk, 73, 107
tracks, for armoured vehicles, 11, 13, 22, 51, 85
trench warfare, effect of, on tank design, 11, 18–19, 22
Tripoli, 72
Tritton, William, 21–2

Tunis, 97

Ukraine, 81
Uman, 81
United States, tanks of, 84–90, 121–31

Valturio, Roberto, 10
Verdun, battle of, 25, 81
Vereeniging, Treaty of, 8
Versailles, Treaty of, 40, 44, 50–1, 55, 61
Vietnam, 112, 117, 138–9
Vigevano, Guido da, 8
Villers-Bretonneux, 31
Vimy Ridge, 27
Vinci, Leonardo da, 10
Volga R., 81
Voroshilov, Klimenti, 51

Waffen-SS, 103
Warsaw, 61
Warsaw rising (1944), 116
Wavell, Field-Marshal Sir Archibald, 69, 73, 76
Wells, H. G., 8, 12, 61
Western Front (1914–18), 18–33
Westminster, Duke of, 20
Weygand, General Maxime, 64–5, 68
Wilson, Lieutenant W. G., 21–2
Wittmann, *Hauptsturmführer* Michel, 103
World Crisis, The, 19

Yom Kippur War (1973), 137–8
Ypres, first battle of, 18
Ypres, third battle of, *see* 'Paschendael'
Yugoslavia, 139

Zhukov, Marshal Georgi, 81, 102
Žižka, John, 9–11